Acknowledgements

KU-005-958

The Chartered Management Institute and the authors wish to acknowledge the financial support and advice provided by the sponsors. The Institute would also like to thank Sir Michael Bichard who chaired the project's Advisory Panel, and his fellow members, for their invaluable guidance, contributions and support which have all helped in bringing this research to fruition.

Project sponsors
- Department for Education and Skills
- Defence Leadership Centre
- Improvement and Development Agency for Local Government
- National College for School Leadership
- The Metropolitan Police Service
- The Training Group Defence Agency

Members of the project's Advisory Panel

Sir Michael Bichard KCB, Chair
Air Commodore David Anderson
Julie Baddeley
Steven Broomhead
Andy Coleman
Harvey Colman
Rhiannon Chapman
Carmel Gallagher
Ram Gidoomal
Dr Elizabeth Haywood
Martin Horton
Jane Kelly
Derek Lewis
Professor Bruce Lloyd
Sir Graham Meldrum
Denise Milani
Professor Leo Murray
Professor Geoff Southworth
David Stevens
Group Captain Tim Winstanley
Sam Younger

The authors owe a considerable debt to the 32 managers from across the public sector that gave up their time to be interviewed in greater depth about the survey findings and their perceptions of leadership.

Special thanks are also due to Nick Rubashow and Richard Daisley at Makrotest Research, who undertook the coding and cross-tabulation of the data.

Foreword

Sir Michael Bichard

In most organisations leadership is the key which unlocks or blocks change. The public service is no different, so the consistently poorer ratings accorded to public sector leaders is a key cause for concern during a period of major reform.

Leading change in the public sector is based on extensive new research undertaken by the Chartered Management Institute with the support of many public sector organisations, and the generous personal contributions and insights from the project's Advisory Panel all with a commitment to *making the difference*.

Through this research we have been seeking to understand better why leaders in the public sector receive low ratings from their followers and to explore the qualities and characteristics most sought after in public leaders. And crucially, what can be done to improve the quality of public leadership?

Some of the findings will strike a familiar chord. Managers are looking for vision, integrity and judgement in their leaders and tend to have a higher regard for their immediate managers than those more senior in the organisation. But other findings are less predictable and merit some closer examination.

Most managers reported that recent reforms had improved service delivery, but many felt that there were too many overlapping initiatives that often blur compelling leadership vision. They are also constrained by the contradictions evident in the commitment on one hand to devolution – one of the Prime Minister's underpinning principles of reform – and the realities which too often restrict the freedom of frontline managers.

Significantly the research demonstrates a very strong correlation between the priority given to leadership development and the level of employee motivation and satisfaction. More worrying is the evidence that most organisations still rely on traditional formalised ways of developing leaders, even though these are often less effective. Equally worrying is the fact that only a quarter of respondents felt that the development budget was adequate and only half of Chief Executives had a personal development plan.

When managers were asked to identify the key public leadership qualities, very few gave a priority to innovation or developing strong relationships with politicians, whilst less than half mentioned partnership working notwithstanding the fragmented nature of governance in the 21st century.

Alongside my colleagues on the Advisory Panel, I believe these findings should cause those who are responsible for public service reform to pause and reflect, and I hope they will then act to benefit from some of the leadership lessons here.

Sir Michael Bichard KCB,
Rector, The London Institute
and former Permanent
Secretary at the Department for
Education and Employment

Chairman, Leading change
in the public sector
project Advisory Panel

May 2003

Contents

Introduction

Overview

This research project provides a reality check among almost 1,900 public sector managers, mostly at middle and junior level, as they face the daily pressures of the public reform agenda. They have shared their attitudes to, and opinions of, current leadership performance in the public sector.

It follows on from a major study into the nature of leadership in UK organisations carried out in 2001 by the Chartered Management Institute in association with the think-tank Demos, on behalf of the Council for Excellence in Management and Leadership. In that report *Leadership: the challenge for all?*, the quality of leadership in UK organisations did not receive high ratings, and public sector organisations received the lowest rating of all.

The new project was designed to examine in more detail the reasons behind the low ratings given to the quality of public sector leadership and to identify the barriers to achieving effective reform. Its primary objectives were to identify and examine the experiences, attitudes and behaviours of public sector managers in terms of:

- The extent of the influence of a unique ethos, value system and environment on leadership attributes and structures in the public sector

- The impact of performance improvement initiatives in the public sector

- The key attributes sought in public sector leaders and measuring the extent to which they are demonstrated

- The extent of development opportunities for potential public sector leaders

Research method

The main focus of the project is a comprehensive quantitative survey among a sample of Chartered Management Institute members drawn from those currently employed in:

- Central government

- Local government

- Health

- Education

- Armed Forces (Army, Navy, RAF)

- Fire service

- Police

Its aim is to provide a different dimension from other case studies and structural analyses for understanding public sector leadership issues. 1,890 practising public sector managers replied to a postal survey sent to a stratified random sample of Institute members in November 2002.

The quantitative findings were then complemented by a series of 32 detailed personal interviews carried out by telephone with individual managers in January/February 2003.

Project context

The public sector is highly diverse in character, governance and size. Its boundaries have changed in recent years and will undoubtedly change again as a steadily stronger consumer culture, rising living standards and a more diverse society lead to greater expectations of responsiveness, reliability and accessibility.

As in the private sector, public organisations face pressures to adapt and innovate to keep up with the best performers. Nonetheless some features clearly distinguish it from the private sector – the political context, funding arrangements, lack of market competition, the pressure to collaborate across different organisations and the ethos of public service.

Reform of the public services is not a new idea. Nor is private sector involvement. Governments have in the past implemented a variety of reforms, including privatisation of nationalised industries and the establishment of the Next Steps agencies under Margaret Thatcher, as well as the initiation of the Citizen's Charter and the extension of market testing and contracting under John Major. During his first term, Tony Blair launched the Modernising Government programme, while his most recent paper *Reforming our public services: principles into practice* (March 2002), identified the following four underpinning principles of reform:

- Establishing a **national framework of standards** and accountability for the delivery of high quality services and effective community leadership

- Within this framework **devolution** to local councils to encourage diversity and creativity giving them the freedom they need to respond to, and meet the needs of, their communities

- Building local capacity in recognition of the need for **flexibility at the frontline** to exploit the opportunities the Government is opening up, and to deliver improved services and effective leadership

- **More choice** for customers with access to an alternative supplier where performance falls below acceptable standards.

Scope of the report   Leadership is a complex and contested subject that can be interpreted in many ways. We have found that people tend to mix their perceptions of the concept of leadership as a specific role in an organisational process, with the characteristics of leadership as displayed by individuals. This survey looks at these various dimensions of leadership.

The **first** section deals with leadership as an organisational process and the macro-climate in terms of the specific public ethos and environment affecting behaviours and values.

The **second** section explores the specific improvement tools and performance initiatives that are being used across public service organisations as the agents for leading change.

The **third** section explores leadership as a set of individual characteristics and skills. It examines the micro-climate of leadership through the lens of the followers and those who have firsthand experience of public sector leadership. It also identifies how managers at all levels can be developed to become effective change agents.

Key Findings and Conclusions

Positive impact
- Nearly six in ten managers report major reforms in the past three years that have directly improved service delivery.

Emerging public sector leadership skills set
- Clarity of vision (66 per cent), integrity (52 per cent) and sound judgement (50 per cent) are the key personal attributes sought from public leaders by their followers. However only about 30 per cent of respondents see these behaviours demonstrated within their own organisation.

- There is a pressing need for public sector managers to develop the ability to build and manage effective relationships both with politicians and across a diverse range of organisations. The research shows that still less than 50 per cent recognise partnership working as a key public leadership skill, while under a quarter (23 per cent) appreciate the importance of developing skills to manage the political dimension.

- Managers in the survey identify communication skills, engaging employees with the vision and creating an enabling culture, as the top three skills they expect of public leaders in general. Yet only a third can see these skills in their own top team. Delivering joined-up solutions and working smarter not harder, means that leaders need more than ever to reaffirm workplace commitment to creation of public value. People are more inclined to support reform that they help create themselves, while resisting that which is forced upon them.

Lack of creativity and innovation
- The lack of creativity and innovation perceived within top teams and line managers is compounded by the low ratings given to leading innovation as a desirable skill in public sector leaders (only 20 per cent of managers included innovation as important). The reform agenda will be impeded if leaders and managers fail to respond to the need for new and more flexible ways of working and thinking.

- Many respondents refer to the emphasis on standards, targets and procedures as a barrier to imaginative management and leadership. The tensions must be resolved between the need for greater creativity and modernisation and the degree of regulation required to improve standards and quality.

Frontline exposure creates spark for better morale
- Citing challenges of inadequate resources and manpower, issues of work-life balance and increased responsibilities, nearly four in ten public sector managers report that employee satisfaction and motivation has shown a decrease over the past three years.

- However, those who experience greater engagement with the local community and who have had direct public involvement in service delivery, reported higher levels of individual enthusiasm and satisfaction from "making the difference".

Devolving accountabilities and managerial autonomy

- Despite promises of more local autonomy, around one in five managers feel their power to influence political decisions has lessened since 1999. Many organisations have devolved responsibilities, but too few distribute real authority or budgetary control. Many procedures are still in place that restrict the freedom of frontline managers to take risks and develop new solutions.

Long term investment in leadership development pays dividends

- The research findings show a significant positive relationship between the organisational priority given to leadership development and the level of employee motivation and satisfaction. Where a low priority was given to leadership development the overall net change in employee satisfaction over the past three years is minus 33. In contrast, where there is high priority given to leadership development, the net change in employee satisfaction is plus 23.

Leadership development priorities

- The survey reveals that only 33 per cent of public sector managers rate the leadership demonstrated by their most senior management team as high quality, with two thirds reporting either low or medium quality leadership. They were more positive however about the abilities of their own line manager, with 44 per cent being rated highly.

- Although a wide and varied range of training activities is taking place, the majority of managers perceive a low priority being placed on leadership development in their organisation.

- Only a quarter of respondents can claim their organisational budget for developing leaders is adequate, and only half of Chief Executives report that they have a personal development plan in place.

- Organisations are still tending to rely on traditional and formalised methods of developing their leaders, whereas effective methods include those which focus on the impact of individual behaviours and which build in time for reflection and feedback.

Performance improvement

- A wide and varied range of initiatives is in place, particularly Investors in People, ISO 9001 and EFQM, but initiative overload is common. Managers identify the key barriers to implementation as sheer pressure of work (63 per cent), insufficient finance (46 per cent) and the time consuming/bureaucratic nature of such approaches (46 per cent).

- Improvement programmes are also perceived by many working within the public sector as overlapping and contradicting each other. There is a pressing need to prioritise and clarify outcomes, while at the same time accepting that initiatives are no substitute for a compelling organisational vision.

- The key benefit of successful performance initiatives is an enhanced focus on client needs (cited by 57 per cent of managers). Here the research also provides an insight into future priorities. Organisations need to focus on developing practical frameworks that place service users and local citizens at the centre of the change agenda.

Recommendations

Building leadership capacity within organisations

- Every organisation within the public sector needs to review and examine our key finding that effective leadership development is the key to leading effective change.

- Organisations need to do more to identify opportunities for leadership which are not tied to formal management positions. Many may have missed the chance to give people practice and confidence through managing specific projects, or leading processes, with the appropriate recognition and rewards.

- Leaders themselves must prioritise their own on-going learning and personal development, and make such learning a part of the example they set to their followers. Given the short-term pressures faced by many leaders, specialist support or coaching programmes that emphasise communication and enabling skills will be particularly helpful in creating the clarity of vision required to achieve long-term change.

Developing public sector leadership skills

- Greater priority needs to be given to developing leaders with the capacity to manage the political dimension. They need an ability to see and communicate the big picture, make connections, be credible with different groups and broker relevant political and strategic relationships. Effective routes include mentoring and working across different environments.

- Rewards for creativity and innovation need to be developed, particularly where managers have been stifled by public sector structures and regulations. Rewards alongside greater devolution of responsibilities and accountabilities for risk will encourage innovative solutions to local problems.

- Greater public involvement requires the capacity for open communication, consultation and dialogue with service users and citizens in general. This new requirement must be included within both development and evaluation activities.

A shared agenda

- More value could be achieved from the specific leadership initiatives across the public sector by learning to work and develop together and by sharing knowledge and experiences. Managers within central Government have an important role in co-ordinating and supporting best practice and local initiatives.

- Increased public scrutiny and sustained media attention create extra pressures on leaders responsible for setting and achieving targets. To counter unrealistic expectations, those developing policy and targets need to reconnect with the frontline and listen to those directly engaged in the provision of services.

- Responsibility for driving up standards should ideally lie closest to those responsible for delivery, and solutions should be designed and maintained by the professionals themselves.

- There must be a revitalisation of the values agenda associated with a commitment to public service and the concept of professional responsibility. Authority needs to be distributed throughout organisations so that all employees have the freedom and are trusted to make a difference. Government at all levels, professional institutions and those responsible for training and development share an obligation to take this forward.

1 A reforming culture – exploring ethos and environment

1.1 The context of change

In theory, with more resources and more freedom promised we should be witnessing a radical turnaround in public sector performance. But in practice, although our survey has revealed good news in terms of a strong focus on improved service delivery, experience of successful cultural changes is still patchy.

The survey revealed that overall 56 per cent of managers claimed that their organisation has undergone a major reform that had directly improved service delivery over the past three years. In contrast, 36 per cent of managers claimed not to have experienced major reforms, while eight per cent admitted that they did not know.

Base: 1890 respondents	Major reform experienced %	No major reforms experienced %
All	56	36
Central government	64	30
Local government	64	29
Health	63	30
Education	42	48
Forces	42	45

Table 1
Experience of major reforms by sector

While some have embraced this new reforming culture, it has not been universally welcomed. Some managers are resisting what they describe as *"change for change's sake"*, which they perceive as being driven by central political demands rather than for the benefit of either employees or the community. Other managers are holding firm to their public sector values of making a difference at the local level, independent from the perceived "nannying" clutches of the centre. As one respondent noted:

"Our local reforms are a closely guarded secret...." (NHS Trust)

Whereas other managers are rising more positively to the challenges created by the desire for continual improvement and constant change:

"Higher education is a tougher world than it was 10 years ago, but it is satisfying and people also have to realise that it's not easier elsewhere. Arguably morale is much better than it is in comparable organisations. However, you no longer join the world of higher education for a quiet life, imagining there to be less pressure." (HE Institution)

Change clearly also affects the private and voluntary sectors, but what we wanted to explore was whether there is a unique public sector culture that impacts on the ability to lead change. It is helpful to understand whether by drilling down into the cultural context of the public sector, we can develop a better understanding of why some changes are successful and also what barriers need to be overcome.

1.2 Changes in organisational culture and values

Managers reported significant changes in organisational culture across the public sector, as demonstrated in the table below. In line with the public service reform agenda, there has been a perceived cultural shift in terms of the new focus on delivery and the end user across the public sector.

However, there are considerable differences in the type of cultural change experienced relative to the context of each particular service. It is therefore more meaningful to look at managers' experiences by sector.

Base: 1890 respondents	All	Central govt.	Local govt.	Health	Education	Forces
Focus on delivery targets	+87	+85	+93	+88	+83	+79
Forming relationships with strategic partners	+77	+76	+87	+75	+75	+64
Accountability	+72	+64	+68	+78	+70	+78
Responsiveness to clients	+64	+72	+75	+72	+62	+40
Working for the public good	+53	+58	+64	+59	+35	+42
Public involvement in service design/delivery	+51	+43	+73	+45	+65	+37
Improved client satisfaction	+50	+55	+58	+54	+49	+33
Ethics/integrity	+39	+34	+35	+37	+20	+56
Influence/involvement of elected authority members	+27	+19	+43	+30	+18	+8
Employee satisfaction/motivation	-3	-2	-8	+2	-15	+10

Table 2
Perceived change in culture and values by sector (net change over past three years)

Public organisations have had to change emphasis over the past three years in order to meet increased public expectations. Over half of survey respondents have experienced greater public involvement in service design and delivery since 2000, while a third report an increase in the influence and involvement of elected members. It is noticeable that local government has experienced the highest perceived increase in the level of public engagement.

1.3 Delivery and creating public value

It is clear that the overriding change across the public sector over the past three years has been the focus on meeting targets. In the qualitative interviews with managers, it was clearly acknowledged that the climate of managing by centrally devised targets and performance indicators has had a positive impact in terms of driving up performance and achieving greater efficiencies. However, there was also a clear sense of unease about whether the targets were reflecting local needs. This is seen in the perception that the levels of client satisfaction and responsiveness to clients have not risen in line with the achievement of delivery targets (see Table 2).

One of the interviewees commented accordingly:

"It is about achieving a balance between standardisation (control) and diversity (autonomy). The pressure to meet published standards reduces the freedom of business units. Accountability should not be confused with control or compliance. Private business has the freedom to make its decisions on the basis of what works in the marketplace, not on the basis of what is in the public interest." (City Council)

There is now a growing appreciation and understanding within central Government that public sector reform should also aim to build on creating public value, through the much harder management and leadership of the unique public sector culture and ethos. It is by engaging hearts and minds of employees and by building on individuals' professional attitudes and belief systems, that increased public value and commitment to the community is being developed. This is in contrast to earlier phases of reform that were much more sharply focused on cost reduction and managing inputs and outputs to demonstrate greater efficiencies and value for money.

From the low employee satisfaction ratings in Table 2 and as reported in many of the interviews, it is clear that the focus on targets has been to the detriment of building value through engaging the enthusiasm of employees. There is also an apparent correlation between the ratings given to ethos and employee satisfaction. The Forces have the highest rating for ethics/integrity (a net change of plus 56 per cent) and also the highest rating for employee satisfaction (a net change of plus 10 per cent). Indeed, the values held by the vast majority of Forces personnel (loyalty and commitment to service) are essential to its capacity to deliver results. In contrast, education has the lowest net change in ethics/integrity (plus 20 per cent), which may have produced a correspondingly low rating for employee satisfaction (minus 15 per cent).

The increased focus on delivery targets has been particularly felt by those in more senior roles as shown in Table 3. There is a striking divergence between the positive changes perceived by Chief Executives and Directors and the lower ratings given by more junior managers. This indicates that the most senior managers and leaders have more to do in terms of engaging their teams. It appears that change management approaches, based around principles more conducive to greater devolution and distributed powers, which use leadership, communication and persuasion to change attitudes and gain consent, are not yet being used as extensively as they could.

With a greater focus on public involvement and working in strategic partnerships, leaders need to do more to offer a compelling vision and narrative to their employees, partners and public. These narratives need to make sense of the challenges that public sector organisations face and reaffirm a commitment to creation of public value through making a tangible difference in the communities they serve.

Base: 1890 respondents	Net change	CE/Director	Senior	Middle	Junior
Focus on delivery targets	+ 87	+ 91	+ 90	+85	+77
Forming relationships with strategic partners	+ 77	+ 85	+ 79	+ 75	+ 65
Accountability	+ 72	+ 82	+ 72	+71	+67
Responsiveness to clients	+ 64	+ 72	+ 69	+61	+56
Working for public good	+ 53	+ 51	+ 54	+56	+48
Public involvement in service delivery/design	+ 51	+ 58	+ 51	+51	+39
Improved client satisfaction	+ 50	+60	+50	+47	+42
Ethics/integrity	+ 39	+39	+38	+38	+34
Influence of elected members	+ 27	+32	+26	+27	+19
Employee satisfaction/motivation	- 3	+17	-2	-6	-34

Table 3
Perceived change in culture and values by management level (net change over past three years)

Personal Perspective

Conflicting priorities and the need for clarity of vision

By David Stevens, Chief Constable, Essex Police

For me, the research identifies two complementary themes that underscore the nature of the challenge facing those of us who are committed to delivering improvement in the public sector. The most frequent barriers to change for senior managers are: clash with other initiatives, emphasis on short-term goals, bureaucracy, work pressures and insufficient finance. At the same time the most valued attribute in senior leadership is clarity of vision. The connection is powerful, at a time when our staff are most in need of clear guidance on what is to be achieved and what their contribution to progress should be, their senior managers are unable to provide that clarity because of the confusion of priorities that surround the public sector.

This confusion is not new; it is inherent in public service where multiple stakeholders have conflicting demands on services, which are themselves necessarily limited by resources. Such a conflict rarely exists in the private sector where managers can take strategic decisions about markets and customers, which can define the service parameters and give clarity of purpose. This complexity makes management in the public sector different and perhaps inherently more challenging and it certainly requires a different skill set. Whilst the survey shows that across the public sector many of the private sector management initiatives have been implemented the fact that several are identified as having low levels of impact must force us to question their relevance to the public sector.

I have found clear echoes of this dilemma in Essex Police where the issue of conflicting priorities and the need for clarity of vision have been a constant challenge. I believe the challenge is being met by starting with effective public consultation, not only on priorities but also on core issues such as the policing style for the County. The early and frequent involvement of staff either directly or through staff associations in policy making, planning and objective setting not only ensures that operational issues are recognised but also gives commitment to the final product. Effective planning has to include not only the identification of priorities but also the budget, business process and human implications.

Performance management concentrates on the priorities and measures progress not only at County and local level but also down to individual level through a Personal Development Plan. Finally, communication has to be relentless and through all available routes – personal, written and technological. The resulting improvement in performance and high levels of public satisfaction are, I believe, strongly linked to a real understanding of what Essex Police is trying to deliver and a clear understanding of the vital part played by every individual in achieving that goal.

1.4 Trust and motivation

A key challenge faced across the public sector is how to engender the professionalism of managers' personal commitment to their particular public communities, and to use it to build a climate that inspires enthusiasm and trust. However, the public sector does not have a monopoly on the service ethos and working for the public good, and a reliance on employees to be driven by such attitudes can lead to inefficiency. No one ethos is always appropriate and the ethos of particular services needs to be developed through engagement with the frontline workers and the end users of the service, whether patients, students or citizens.

According to the survey findings, employee motivation and satisfaction have decreased in overall terms during the past three years. There are significant differences between the sectors, with education suffering from the poorest motivation, and the Forces and health experiencing a net increase in motivation (see Table 2).

Interviewees from the education sector urged caution however on interpreting the statistics as a story of doom and gloom:

Consideration of aggregate data on staff morale requires intelligent and critical interpretation. The unions tend to give a negative picture overall. However, the Institution is a positive environment, where people are developed, more staff are being employed and there is now far greater engagement with the local economy and community. The majority of staff are very proud to work in a place such as a higher education college, doing a job that pays a reasonable salary and teaching subjects that they are passionate about. (Higher Education)

A manager within an NHS Trust revealed a mixed picture regarding morale:

Depends on where you look – but generally morale is low because of access targets. Morale was at its lowest pre-merger, and it has taken 12 months to get the new structures in place; it is therefore now improving. The morale among the nursing staff is still low, because of the relentless pressures on frontline staff. There is no longer a quieter summer period and downtime, which makes it difficult to catch up with administration etc. There is still the problem of not enough staff to deliver the desired activities.

Significantly, those who reported greater engagement with the local community and who were directly involved with the public in the delivery of services, also reported higher personal morale. The closeness to the delivery enables staff to see how they can implement solutions at a local level. While there has been some devolution from the centre to enable greater distributed authority, there is still considerable tension between the central and local delivery agendas which are holding back reforms and individuals' enthusiasm.

When exploring in more depth the values driving those working in the public sector, the most repeated comment was the desire "to make a difference". The majority of the frustrations expressed were either the lack of resources or insufficient managerial autonomy.

It is also evident that the perceived job security is a key attraction for those working in the public sector. Despite reporting poor morale and motivation, there is still a strong loyalty pull to the employer, in perceived contrast to those working in the private sector.

Base: 1890 respondents	Better %	Same %	Worse %	Don't know %
Perceived job security	59	27	9	5
Loyalty to employer	48	31	15	6
Motivation	23	34	36	6
Morale	15	35	44	6

Table 4
Perceptions of public sector values relative to the private sector

1.5 Management autonomy

Two assumptions underpin the public management change agenda. One is that better management and leadership would make a difference to public organisations' performance. The other is that "the manager's right to manage" has been undermined by rigid central accountability frameworks and by professional groups/trade unions in many public services.

Much of the reform process has focused on giving more power to managers, at the expense of professional groups, and freeing them from inappropriate political controls. However, in many respects the empowerment of managers has been more rhetoric than reality, and as the following results indicate, there has been an overall net decrease over the past three years in their ability to resist inappropriate political interference.

Base: 1890 respondents	Increased	Same	Decreased	Net change
Aspect of autonomy	%	%	%	%
Setting performance objectives	61	27	11	+50
Ability to create and develop teams	51	36	12	+39
Power to develop strategic alliances	47	38	9	+38
Power to respond to clients' needs	48	35	13	+35
Input into strategy or policy decisions	52	28	19	+33
Budgetary autonomy	27	44	23	+4
Power to influence political decisions	18	49	22	-4
Power to resist inappropriate political interference	11	49	33	-22

Table 5
Perceived change in
degree of autonomy over
past three years

In many cases there has been a growth in apparent autonomy: managers have the ability to set performance objectives, create and develop their own teams, and to develop strategic alliances. However, in practice, these have rarely related to increases in actual autonomy at a fundamental level – finances and the ability to hire and fire has still not been devolved to the local level.

The majority of managers can set their own performance objectives, but only in terms of either how they will contribute to national targets or at best, the achievement of their organisation's local targets. Likewise, the perceived increase in the ability to create and develop teams can relate to increases in cross-functional working rather than recruiting new members. The ability to develop their teams is also dependent on their particular organisation's delegation of budgets for development, and there is a reported tendency for such budgets to be siphoned off by high performing departments or teams. This is reflected in the fact that managerial control over resources and budgets has increased only marginally, by a net 4 per cent, over the past three years.

The findings on political control, both in terms of the ability to influence decisions and the power to resist inappropriate interference, has reduced significantly since 2000. In service organisations that rely heavily on people to get things done, the control over "people issues" lags significantly behind. Many of the interviewees cited in further detail the problem of providing appropriate rewards and recognition for their teams when pay and promotional issues are still determined centrally. Furthermore in terms of resources, there is still not enough freedom to recruit, promote and manage staff effectively in the light of local needs and labour markets:

"Much still needs to be done to push real fiscal freedoms, with appropriate checks and balances, down to the lower levels. You need to remove the dead hand of the centre which still controls manpower. In industry, you can hire and fire, but public sector managers can't. If you really want to streamline you need to slaughter the sacred cows at the centre, and it is only then that you will really begin to realise the untapped initiative and innovation that exists at the local level." (RAF)

Pay bargaining for some of the largest groups in the public sector – especially in health and education, not to mention the fire brigade, police service and virtually all central government staffing – is still managed from the centre (Government and the Treasury in negotiation with professional associations/unions). The public sector pay policies pursued by the Government are clear enough evidence of this. However it has been argued that despite these overall central controls, local managers have been given discretion over the exact mix of pay and grading in their own organisation. The survey does show that this is happening, but only on a relatively small scale, and managers do not see their control over pay and grading growing significantly.

In the near future, it is unlikely that central Government will surrender effective control over public sector pay, which is both crucial to Government fiscal controls and a major economic lever in its own right. This is why progress on devolving pay control away from Whitehall, pay review bodies and the like, has been very slow in practice and is likely to remain so.

1.6 Political governance

As the table below indicates, respondents claim their ability to resist inappropriate political interference has significantly declined over the past three years.

Base: 1890 respondents	Power to influence political decisions	Power to resist inappropriate political interference
Central government	-5	-22
Local government	9	-12
Health	-21	-49
Education	-19	-27
Forces	-2	-22

Table 6
Perceived change in ability to influence/resist political decisions (net change over past three years)

Many managers identify political prerogatives and central delivery targets as a major driving force for change. Nevertheless there are so many centrally driven initiatives for change that frontline managers claim:

" We are suffering the syndrome of jumping on every latest bandwagon, often with no clear sense of direction as to where the next journey will take us. " (Borough Council)

Respondents and interviewees expressed the need for more freedom to use their initiative and common sense to explore new diverse ways of delivering services, but felt restricted by procedures that are too prescriptive. They also felt that those responsible for setting targets did not always have either the necessary expertise, or sufficient exposure to frontline realities.

Successful target setting should be an iterative process, with sufficient space for those delivering the services to create their own detail. Mavericks and entrepreneurs who are often the necessary catalysts for driving radical reforms, still sit uneasily within cultures driven by the need to meet targets and rigid performance management criteria. Although the untapped sources of innovation are those who deliver frontline services, interviewees vividly described the *"enemy within: a blocking layer of internal bureaucracy"* and *"those cloistered at the centre"*.

Central government may have devolved powers to Executive Agencies, the Regional Development Agencies and non-departmental public bodies, but in many respects this has resulted in the creation of multiple funding streams and an increasing public accountability burden. One manager explained:

" The accountability burden is now excessive and the formal bureaucracy is very heavy. It is right that senior managers have to ensure accountability for public monies and are subject to high level scrutiny, but it has now gone too far. Changes to funding arrangements over recent years mean that income for HE now comes from many different public bodies, such as HEFCE, TTA and DoH, which creates more work. Each stream of funding requires bids and each successful bid then needs to be monitored and accounted for. In Autumn 2001, the HE establishment made 15 bids in 12 weeks – it is almost becoming an industry in itself. For a medium sized HE college, this takes up senior staff time, as to hire consultants would take too long and be too expensive. There is still not enough joined-up thinking centrally and the Departments are competing

internally. There should be single pot funding streams. The HE White Paper has recognised this problem and is making efforts to reduce bureaucracy, and the principle of "earned autonomy" needs to be applied quickly." (Higher Education)

There is a perceived need for public sector managers to develop the ability to build and manage effective relationships both with politicians and across a diverse range of organisations. The series of interviews demonstrated that central government decision-making, and even the work of senior public sector managers, is often remote from frontline delivery. Many managers commented on the distance between those with a direct operational knowledge and those determining central policies.

In the same way that many private sector organisations send their senior managers back to the floor, similar initiatives are being incorporated within Civil Service training and secondment opportunities between departments and service providers. This is also developing through the greater emphasis on partnership working.

However, the evidence from this survey is that the persistent disjunction between political rhetoric and managerial reality is still considerable. Current policies on devolving power are clearly not working adequately, and may even be making the situation worse, by adding intermediate layers of management through the introduction of new agencies.

The proposed solution of offering further freedoms, initially for NHS Hospitals, in terms of foundation status may start addressing this issue by devolving ownership of hospitals from the Department of Health to the local communities. However, the Health Bill published in March 2003 potentially sets out extensive powers for the regulator, which depending on how they are defined in practice, could result in foundation hospitals having less freedom.

Foundation hospitals will be subjected to at least five different types of scrutiny. They will have a governing body of local people; primary care trusts who purchase from them; they will be subject to the Commission for Healthcare Audit and Inspection (CHAI); they will be in the hands of the regulator and they will face a statutory duty to co-operate with other NHS bodies.

Also, on the face of it, foundation hospitals will be able to set their own terms and conditions for staff. However, these freedoms may be no greater than those contained in the "Agenda for Change" – the plan for a more complex (but more flexible) pay system that is currently out to consultation across the NHS.

It is also hoped that the development of effective cross-Departmental Public Service Agreements and single pot funding stream initiatives across a number of Departments and Executive Agencies will simplify the bureaucracy. However, much progress is required in terms of developing flexible models of accountability that can demonstrate value to citizens as overseers of Government, to customers as users of public services, and taxpayers as funders, while at the same time providing the desired local managerial autonomy.

As we shall see later perceptions of the quality of leadership are poor, especially in some sectors like local government and education. The detachment from practical implementation and isolation of policy makers within sectors or in central government was a theme that featured regularly in the qualitative interviews.

As one senior manager from a large government department admitted:

> "They're like a group of people at a dinner party when the lights go out. Instead of fumbling for the matches or trying to find the fuse box, they'd rather sit for hours in the dark discussing policy."

1.7 Challenges of changing cultures

In many ways, it is easier to implement the structures for empowerment – decentralised budgets, control over pay etc – than it is to change attitudes and beliefs which affect how extensively people will use the new structures. As discussed earlier, even achieving structural changes turns out to be far more difficult in the public sector because of its public accountabilities, ethos of equity in provision and the role of politicians.

It is clear that it is difficult to implement cultural changes if those leading the organisation are not seen to be committed to the values inherent in such changes. For instance, the promotion of change can takes place through top-down directives, and this often runs contrary to the philosophy of devolving decision-making to managers.

The performance improvement tools and statutory inspection regimes as discussed in the next section are in some ways an example of this top-down directive and command and control approach to change. While targets and regulations play an important role in driving up standards, it is often an issue of how they have been promoted.

This is not to argue that successful change does not require an initial burst of energy and push from the top, but unless such a top-down initiative is complemented by more participative and collaborative approaches to implementation it is unlikely to be successfully sustained.

This is even more likely to be the case where the changes envisaged are about the decentralisation of responsibility.

The alternative change management approaches based around principles more conducive to greater devolution and distributed powers, which use leadership, communication and persuasion to change attitudes and gain consent, is not yet being used as extensively as it could be.

In terms of the key challenges faced by public sector managers, resources and insufficient manpower is cited as the key barrier to reform, see Table 7 below.

Base: 1890 respondents	All %	Central govt. %	Local govt. %	Health %	Education %	Forces %
Resources/manpower levels	63	55	64	64	51	79
Work/life balance	43	45	40	42	47	51
Increased job responsibilities	40	37	36	44	41	43
Outcomes rather than inputs focus	35	38	39	35	30	27
Statutory inspection regimes	28	11	36	24	46	16
Level of support from above	23	25	20	23	24	24
Career uncertainty	21	30	18	24	16	22
Managing innovation/creativity	18	21	20	20	16	14
Personal growth/development	14	21	8	15	13	15
Delivering services online	9	14	13	4	8	4

Personal Perspective

Leadership and strategy: special challenges for the public sector

By Bruce Lloyd, Professor of Strategic Management,
South Bank University

A key role for leadership in any organisation is to facilitate the development of, and then to encourage commitment to, the organisation's strategy. In this context, it is useful to identify and explore those (overlapping) elements of the process mentioned below that can easily present special challenges for leadership in the public sector in view of its particular ethos and environment.

1 Political influence (both nationally and locally) in both setting agendas and objectives, as well as often being involved in the development of detailed performance indicators, emphasises the need for effective stakeholder management techniques.

2 The volatility of the political agenda in the UK over the past 50 years has made it difficult to establish a basic framework of continuity that is usual for any effective strategy over the long term.

3 The need for radical change is often over emphasised. The experience of the private sector is that such radical changes are defined as unsuccessful in more than 50 per cent of cases. There is often much talk of the need for 'culture change', without the phrase being properly defined.

4 The political elements mentioned above mean the role of the media could often have a disproportionate influence on both perceptions and practicalities.

5 There is often great pressure for 'change' within a context of poorly defined performance indicators. Yet the essence of successful change is for the change to be perceived by those involved as 'progress'. Without this accepted agenda, change is often just driven by personalities and politics.

6 Another issue associated with change is that, in general, the more change the less empowerment. Empowerment programmes are often a major cause of stress as they frequently encourage the delegation of responsibility without providing the necessary authority and management support. A key role of management is to help those who are responsible for implementing change to do their job more effectively; yet it is relatively rare that this support is reflected by the views of their staff.

7 It is often argued that professionals involved in public sector activities tap into a different ('higher') values agenda. Further research is needed to explore values

Continued…

issues in greater depth. The whole subject of the role and nature of 'professionalism' was undermined by the culture of commercialism in the 1980s and it is not easy to see the philosophy of 'public service' being rediscovered as the driving force behind a new approach to professionalism. There is an expectation that the values agenda results in both those at the top and throughout the organisation working to higher standards than those in the private sector, although there is relatively limited evidence to support such a view.

8   There is great emphasis on the need for participation but, while this is incredibly beneficial if well managed, it can raise expectations that create new demands on the leadership and management within the organisation. Most staff do not feel very involved in any strategic planning process, even when it exists explicitly.

9   Many areas of the public sector still have powerful unions, and while it is accepted that unions can provide a valuable role, in many areas their activities have done much to undermine the effectiveness of middle management in many organisations – and it is not easy to break the vicious circles of history. For example, poor management increases the role of the unions, and that increase in power can further undermine the effectiveness of management. At the same time there are examples of union harassment, if not bullying, of middle management.

10 All organisations are increasingly aware of the impact and cost of mistakes (whether it is an accident on the railways or a poor decision in the childcare services) and this can easily result in organisations becoming even more bureaucratic and even more reluctant to innovate. There is also a tendency to try to resolve a wide range of organisational issues, such as diversity, using bureaucratic solutions (more procedures and manuals), rather than emphasising the importance of trust, respect and relationships.

11 There is an emphasis on developing partnerships and strategic alliances; yet these are very management-intensive activities and they benefit from a range of skills that take time to develop. Again this requires appropriate technical knowledge and its application within the context of a relevant values agenda.

12 Resource allocation decisions in a climate where there are not broadly accepted performance indicators can easily become divisive.

Overall the role of leadership, and its link with the development of an effective strategy, is particularly demanding in the public sector for the reasons mentioned above. The successful operation of a public sector organisation, in practice, requires the effective combination of a genuine commitment to a public service values agenda, with a knowledge base of management skills that is, unfortunately, much rarer than we would all like it to be.

1.8 Innovation and intrapreneurship

Disturbingly, the survey indicated that leading the innovation process came very low on managers' desired attributes and qualities for public sector leaders. When asked to indicate the top five skills required by public sector leaders, only 20 per cent of managers identified "leading the innovation process" and even fewer identified the ability to lead innovation as being demonstrated by either their own line manager (16 per cent) or most senior manager (14 per cent).

The detailed interviews revealed that the initiative for innovation is often at the frontline when, at an operational level, managers develop more efficient approaches. Similarly, it was noted that through direct dialogue with customers and the public, new ways of maximising delivery are developed.

One example was given by a former staff nurse who had moved into a corporate management role within an NHS Trust but had perceived the need for building in more innovative thinking around operational problems. Working in strategic partnership with an academic centre, the manager had consequently set up a 3-day programme involving developing entrepreneurial attributes such as "Thinking out of the box" and developing creativity and innovation through specific tools and techniques. One pilot session had taken place with ten managers and clinicians from across the trust. As an initial outcome, nine out of ten could see considerable value from the programme, and only one individual could not cope with the radical development methods used. All of the pilot group were asked to bring a problem and part of the programme was about helping them to develop individual and creative solutions. As part of the longer-term evaluation, the Trust will be examining how they have taken their solutions back to their working environment.

The prevalent culture across the public sector, as often characterised by excessive targets and regulations, is clearly holding back innovation. This was clearly evidenced by the interviews:

"*Our central departments do not recognise innovation, particularly finance. Managers who find innovative ways of doing things tend to get squashed, as that's not the way things have been done in the past. The legal and finance teams are unable to manage the level of risk. Successful risk management can encourage innovation, whereas in our organisation it is more a question of management by risk avoidance.*" (Borough Council)

Innovation and creativity takes place within a framework that is both values driven and reflects a basic commitment to the underlying strategic objectives. The public nature of missed targets or public sector "mistakes", results in an underlying clash between media/political blame culture and the need for a more responsible managerial learning culture. For this to be resolved there needs to be a climate of trust and appropriate management of risk, but partly because of the media intensity on public sector reform, the trust is being eroded and bureaucracy is being used as a defence mechanism. A lack of trust often emerges between managers and specific professionals, and without trust the usual result is more rules, regulations and formal procedures.

Partnership working should be adopted to create new ways of meeting needs collectively and this can only be achieved by new ways of interfacing with service users and communities. But without significant change to the wider systems and top-down target setting, new ways of working will develop only to serve the legacy of the past and former agendas. There are great efforts to involve the public in identifying local issues and possible solutions, but in many cases successful implementation will still require levels of collaboration and agreement far in excess of the way "the system" currently works.

Case Study

**Setting up a new Non-Departmental Public Body
– a success but lessons to be learned**

(Based on a report by a central Government Department's Internal
Audit on the implementation of the NDPB project)

Ministers wanted to move quickly to tackle a failing infrastructure. Following consultation it was decided to establish a new NDPB. This body would promote and facilitate the active engagement of the public, private and voluntary sectors, identify and address areas of market failure, encourage bodies to seek a government licence, and regulate a licensed system.

The task was set up as a project working to the Department's project management guidelines. It had three phases – consultation, response to consultation and Government policy statement, and implementation. The first two phases of the project were managed in house, well controlled and adhered to the Department's guidelines. The consultation was the first Departmental consultation using new Cabinet Office guidelines. Working closely to these procedures a major contentious consultative exercise was successfully completed and radical changes to policy negotiated with other government departments and agencies and the devolved administrations. The more "interesting" phase is implementation.

Implementation phase

This was split into three strands – Policy, Communications and NDPB set-up (premises, IT, recruitment). The responsible Minister took a very hands-on role as Chair of the Implementation Board. The overall project manager was a civil service director (Grade 3). The policy and set up strand leaders were senior civil service managers (Grade 5). A consultant was employed to oversee the communication strand. A further separate consultancy was engaged to provide sophisticated project management skills and coordinate the project. The project team was located within the responsible policy division (the host division).

Delivery

The project was implemented to very tight timescales. The personal involvement of the Minister was a significant factor enabling issues to be thrashed out and decisions taken at short notice. The set up strand, drawing in a team of civil servants with relevant experience and IT project management skills was very sharp. It worked largely to its own plan, rather independently of the other project strands.

Continued...

Significant difficulties occurred in relation to the overall project management and the policy and communications strands. The pace of the project and the pulling together of a 45 strong project team (including a "shadow" team developing the NDPB functions) made it difficult to manage. With hindsight, placing overall project management at Director level was a mistake as the post holder was very stretched dealing with a number of controversial policy issues and running a large Directorate.

The external consultancy, while providing high level support to the Implementation Board, had difficulty at the operational level. It struggled to coordinate the three strands, documentation and budgetary control were deficient and the approach to planning and risk management was not consistent. Its lack of knowledge of the Department's systems and culture had a negative effect. Specialist resources within the Department were not utilised from the beginning and as a result wrong paths were taken. As there was already good quality project management skill in the host division, which was familiar with the project management process, better use could have been made of this with external consultants used on a call off basis rather than full time. Towards the end of the implementation phase, a rough and ready approach needed to be taken to conclude the project, which although falling short of the Department's guidelines, was effective.

Although located within the host division, communication between the project team and the division was given insufficient attention. There was a lack of recognition of the need to fully involve those who would sponsor and work with the NDPB once the project ended. Some staff of the host division felt excluded and that their potential to make a contribution to the success of the project was not valued. There were also difficulties in communication with the Devolved Administrations in Scotland, Wales and Northern Ireland. Again towards the end of the project these issues were recognised and addressed.

Despite these problems, the project can be counted a success having delivered to time and budget. In addition important lessons were learned about how to lead and manage a complex public sector project:

• Clarity and realism are needed about the responsibilities and capacity of project leaders. Dynamic support cannot be provided where leaders have to deal with competing priorities especially if these are politically demanding.

• External consultants are not a panacea. They must operate in an unfamiliar context. Where there are established departmental processes for project management, planning and risk management and budgetary control consultants must work within them. Utilising in house expertise and supplementing it with external consultancy on an "as needed" basis will minimise misunderstandings

Continued…

… from previous page

and facilitate communication within the departmental culture. In this case it would also have enabled a smoother move from policy development to implementation.

- Excellent communication and clearly defined roles and responsibilities are essential in a fast moving and fragmented project environment. It is a great benefit to have the direct involvement of a Minister but this must be accompanied by consistent advice from strand leaders.

2 Improving performance

2.1 Background to key initiatives

Ministerial involvement in details of local provision can be traced to the Citizen's Charter of ten years ago, with the publication of league tables and the creation of the national curriculum in schools. Whitehall involvement has increased substantially since 1999, and a main theme has been public service orientation – a renewed focus on citizens and customers, with an emphasis on quality of service, consultation and involvement. However the practice has often emphasised narrow concepts of cost efficiency, although some other gains are seen as more positive – not least the clarification of accountabilities and responsibilities.

2.2 Managerial views on key initiatives

One of the key objectives of the survey was to examine the extent and impact of performance improvement initiatives from the perspective of the individuals who are expected to implement such schemes.

Respondents reported a wide range of initiatives with the well-established Investors in People, service delivery targets and inspection regimes the most common at around 70 per cent penetration. The next significant clustering around the 30 per cent share, related to two of the key quality standards ISO 9001 and EFQM, both of which are also quite familiar to many public sector organisations.

Base: 1890 respondents Improvement initiative	In place %
Investors in People	72
Service delivery targets	68
Statutory inspection regimes	64
ISO 9001	29
Business Excellence Model (EFQM)	29
Individual performance-related pay (PRP)	29
Charter Mark	22
Beacon recognition	14
Group-based performance pay	7
BS EN 12973 (value management)	1

Table 8
Improvement initiatives in place across public sector

Beacon recognition is a comparatively new initiative compared with the others, and is more likely to have been won in local government organisations (especially London/Metropolitan Boroughs – 37 per cent, and county councils – 30 per cent).

Investors in People (IIP) is probably among the best known and one of the longest established quality frameworks. Since 1990, more than 29,000 organisations have achieved recognition. The survey results confirm its dominant positioning, ranging from 95 per cent uptake among the Forces, to 80 per cent in central government and 72 per cent in local government.

Sector	Most used initiatives	Greatest impact	Least impact
Central govt.	IIP (80%) Service delivery targets (73%) Individual PRP (70%)	Service delivery targets	Individual PRP
Local govt.	Service delivery targets (88%) Statutory inspection (73%) IIP (72%)	Statutory inspection regimes	IIP
Health	Service delivery targets (77%) Statutory inspection (63%) IIP (50%)	Service delivery targets	IIP
Education	Statutory inspection (77%) IIP (64%) Service delivery targets (50%)	Statutory inspection regimes	IIP
Forces	IIP (95%) Statutory inspection (50%) ISO 9001 (48%)	IIP	IIP

Table 9
Usage and impact of
initiatives by sector

Statutory inspection is most prevalent in the education sector overall (77 per cent compared with 64 per cent overall). Managers working in schools were particularly likely to report experience of inspection regimes (86 per cent). Service delivery targets are already in place for 88 per cent of local government managers and for 77 per cent of health managers.

The defined nature of service delivery targets and the non-discretionary aspect of inspection regimes make it more likely that they would have a tangible impact on individuals as shown in Table 10.

Initiatives	%
Statutory inspection regimes	43
Service delivery targets	35
Business Excellence Model	17
ISO 9001 (quality)	16
IIP	15

Table 10
Performance
improvement initiatives –
with greatest impact

Survey respondents, however, reported the difficulties they faced on a daily basis, describing the demands that targets and measurement placed on the organisation.

"The number of inspection regimes is unbelievable. This year alone we have been audited externally and internally by Charter Mark, IIP, Clinical Negligence Scheme for trusts, Commission for Health Inspection, special audit for waiting lists. Each requires boxes of evidence, leaving managers no time to manage." (NHS Trust)

"More effort is involved in producing performance statistics than actual performance improvement. Targets are constantly changing both in volume and areas of performance." (District Council)

"Performance improvement initiatives tend to be mechanistic and prescribed from above, thus reducing initiative and professional discretion. Most time is spent firefighting and form filling and meeting audit requirements." (Further Education)

Busy, but under-resourced, public sector managers are also suspicious about management initiatives perceived as simply adding new rhetoric to existing processes.

"Our leadership now has a reputation for following the flavour of the month." (Executive Agency)

"Increases bureaucracy without an increase in resources." (Prisons)

Indeed after workload and funding issues, Table 11 shows that "Faddism" is one of the key contributory factors to the failure of improvement programmes according to 46 per cent of managers, while a similar percentage were critical of the detailed bureaucracy they entail.

Base: 1890 respondents	%
Work pressures	63
Insufficient finance	46
Perceived as just another management fad	46
Too time-consuming and bureaucratic	46
Emphasis on short-term goals	41
Clash with other initiatives	36
Resistance from employees	30
Lack of training	26
Lack of commitment from the top	25

Table 11
Barriers to
implementation of
performance
improvement initiatives

Around a third of respondents cited clashes with other initiatives as problematic, and this was illustrated neatly by one interviewee who commented:

"Too many initiatives in too short a time has devalued the benefit that could have been gained." (Fire Service)

Furthermore the managers who were interviewed referred to their struggles in prioritising improvement programmes that are perceived to overlap and sometimes even to contradict each other.

Public sector managers overall were most likely to cite IIP as having had the least impact within their organisation, as shown below:

Initiative	%
IIP	34
Individual performance-related pay	32
Beacon recognition	32
Group-based performance payments	23
Charter Mark	20

Table 12
Performance improvement initiatives – with least impact

While it is fair to say that the qualitative comments about IIP from respondents were also generally lukewarm, it might be that "familiarity has bred contempt" among managers due to IIP's relative maturity as a performance initiative. It might also be that the organisational issues it was introduced to improve are now more fully understood and less problematic creating diminishing returns. Indeed some interviewees described just that situation:

"It no longer has a great impact in terms of changing practice as it is really a recognition/badge as the practices are already in place. It helps to focus minds, however, and provides a reminder across the organisation as occasionally there are some departments that need an additional carrot or stick." (Higher Education)

"IIP has had the least impact because the culture has always been underpinned by its principles e.g. encouraging people to develop. It has, however, made people think to get things written down in a more formal manner for the future." (NHS Trust)

"Recognition was almost a confirmation of what we've been doing well for 80 or 90 years. We have such a strong emphasis on training and development we're almost driven by the central principles, but it's still nice to have." (RAF)

Other managers were more critical however:

"Mainly seen as ticking boxes and "coaching" for interviews so that a plaque can be put in reception." (Higher Education)

"All well and good to achieve it but a bit of window dressing – as we haven't got the funds to actually do the training." (Metropolitan Borough)

"My council has the badge and everyone has personal development interviews, but at the end of the day there is no budget for training, therefore its overall impact is limited." (Borough Council)

Despite these reservations, such an established quality tool **can** go some way towards providing more externally focused information about relative performance and offering suggestions for improvement.

Personal Perspective

The politics of performance

By Professor Leo Murray, Cranfield School of Management

There can be little doubt that the policy of ensuring value from public service and expenditure is valuable and essential. Over recent years, the UK has become one of the leaders in developing performance systems and measurement frameworks and concepts in an ongoing drive to embed improvements in efficiency.

An ethos of measuring and communicating performance, transparency and accountability has long been a mainstay of a sector that must account for expenditure and management of the public purse. Government departments, Executive Agencies and local government representatives are now seeking more robust and appropriate means of measuring and managing performance. The stimuli for this effort are wide and varied, but certainly include Public Service Agreements, Best Value initiatives and the Spending Review.

But perhaps what is different in this era of 'joined up Government' is the sheer volume of measures that now inform public sector work and decision-making.

In the quest for knowledge, accountability and performance improvements, it is easy to end up measuring everything but learning little.

Many public sector organisations collect enormous amounts of data from a variety of sources and also appear to be at different stages in the evolution and development of their thinking about performance measurement and management.

Key questions to be answered both through the ongoing work of the Centre for Business Performance at Cranfield and through the Institute's research project include:

How does the public sector make sense of all of these measures to drive forward improvements?

Are the right measures in place to highlight and deliver these criteria?

What are the drivers for effective performance measures?

It should be remembered however that public sector outcomes should not necessarily be measured around the same frameworks and criteria as those in the private sectors, where cost, financial imperative and shareholder value hold sway. The focus instead is on valuing service and service improvements.

2.3 Public Service Agreements

The cornerstone of the Government's approach to clarifying public service objectives and setting firm standards is the system of Public Service Agreements (PSAs) established in 1998. They are negotiated between the Treasury and spending departments at each Spending Review. Objectives are matched by targets stating the outcomes and outputs that will be delivered in return for funding.

Although PSA targets have played a key role in achieving change, for example in relation to waiting time in hospitals and literacy and numeracy in schools, by the Government's own admission only 30 of the 130 public service agreements (PSA) it set in 2000 have been achieved. Furthermore according to a study of nearly 600 PSAs, some 40 per cent set in 1998 have failed or are on course to fail, and 75 per cent of targets set in 2000 are in the same state.

By March 2003 it had been announced that the number of formal targets had been halved from 250 to 125, and that in future, goals will be outlined in policy statements without the due date necessarily being made public. This will still mean a large degree of top-down government, despite pledges of commitment to decentralisation.

2.4 Best Value

This is a performance framework introduced by the Government in 1999. Replacing compulsory competitive tendering, it requires local authorities to deliver services to clear standards by the most economic, efficient and effective means available. Authorities are expected to achieve continuous improvement in all their services. Most are now more open about their performance and are using Best Value to ask challenging questions of themselves, and to ensure that they are more in touch with the needs and wishes of service users and council tax payers. The best authorities show that lasting and relevant service improvement is rooted in ongoing dialogue with service users and the wider community. Inspection and audit of Best Value have undoubtedly provided an important external challenge to councils. Many of the respondents who reported that their organisation had introduced major reforms which had improved service delivery (56 per cent) were generally positive about the role of Best Value in this regard:

"Best Value has forced the pace on a number of critical areas and has obliged managers to ask some very fundamental questions."
(District Council)

"Best Value strategic reviews of services resulted in changes in both management and operational structures leading to improved services."
(Unitary Authority)

"A painful but useful exercise as, if we were left to our own devices, many reforms would not naturally happen." (Borough Council)

Elected members in particular often welcome the opportunity for challenge and critical review that inspection has provided.

"The influence of members has increased, but this is a good thing as it provides a reality check. There needs to be transparency and openness." (District Council)

Interviewees had experienced some difficulties, however, in aligning members who had been used to a "political" culture before with the stronger customer focus required from the new "service" model. Clearly many, if not all, councils and authorities have learned important lessons about how they can improve services from local people. But many still need to go further and need to form a clear focus on what matters to the people they serve.

"We are actively seeking the views of customers on service provision and responding by acting on them." (Unitary Authority)

"Cross-banding and cross sectoral delivery of services. Greater consultation and involvement of customers and staff." (Unitary Authority)

Personal Perspective

Local Government Improvement Programme (LGIP)

By Carmel Gallagher, Improvement and Development Agency for Local Government

Local government is big business. It spends over £75 billion in public money each year and employs 2.5 million people in the UK. Local councils face a number of challenges, in a social and political context where change is an imperative not an option. The debate as to whether the statutory inspection regime has significantly improved performance in local government is inconclusive, because the impact of intervention is still little understood through conventional methods. Research indicates that the peer review process, which is the cornerstone of LGIP, has enabled local authorities to achieve significant improvement. The LGIP was set up in 1999 by IDeA (the Improvement and Development Agency) in conjunction with the then DETR, the Audit Commission and the Local Government Association (LGA). More than 150 councils have already undertaken LGIP.

The basis of the programme is peer review, where a high-level team visits, assesses performance against the "ideal" benchmark and makes recommendations for the improvement plan. The implementation of the plan is then monitored over a period.

The benchmark centres on three areas in which a fully effective local authority needs to demonstrate a high level of competence:

- Leadership
- Democratic and Community Engagement, and
- Performance Management.

Councils have reported that LGIP created an impetus for change in their organisations. There were numerous examples of change identified as a result of the council taking forward the recommendations of the peer review team. These include radical restructuring to bring systems more in line with service requirements, more effective political management arrangements, community consultation, partnership working and renewed energy and commitment among senior management teams.

Corporate recognition of the need to address issues and commitment to improve from individuals, members and management team were the main reasons given for improvement achieved – underlining the importance of leadership in the change management process. Clarity of task, the credibility of the review team, and new legal requirements were contributory factors in achieving change.

Local government needs to be open to change and to challenge perceptions, while recognising that for many difficult issues there may not always be an optimum

Continued...

... from previous page

solution. Nor should it be assumed that the private sector is good and the public sector inefficient by definition. Clearly sophisticated leadership skills are vital, including communication, change management and corporate working aptitude. For senior managers as much as for members, "political" competence is important. Managers need to understand the reasons why change initiatives fail and recognise the complexity of culture change.

Crucially, this constellation of necessary skills suggests that councils, in common with other large organisations, need to look anew at procedures that have in the past tended to see senior managers rise through the ranks on the basis of their professional and technical expertise. This route creates particular "professional" paradigms for strategic thinking which can result in a curbing of the creativity and innovation that is crucial if councils are to become learning organisations.

2.5 Comprehensive Performance Assessment (CPA)

There are 467 councils in the UK and over 11,000 town, parish and community councils. CPA was introduced in the Government's White Paper *Strong Local Leadership: Quality Public Services* (2001). It is the cornerstone of changes to the performance management framework for local government and retains the potential to be a major driver for change in central/local government relations. The CPA asks key questions:

- Is this a well-run organisation?

- Has it the capacity to change and improve?

- Does it do the important things properly?

The Comprehensive Performance Assessment carried out in 2002 on top-tier local authorities is now being run on the 250 second-tier district councils. The Audit Commission graded 22 councils after the 2002 exercise as excellent, 54 as good, 39 fair, 22 weak and 13 poor after assessing 150 authorities over 12 months. Inspectors assessed each of the councils by analysing reports from a variety of inspectorates including social services, Ofsted, housing and Best Value reports.

Excellent councils tend to have political leadership that is strategic, clear and focused in its priorities. This is successfully communicated to officials and percolates down to council staff. Councils that are performing well receive benefits from central government in terms of reduced audit and inspection regimes as well as increased flexibility and borrowing freedoms. Those that are performing poorly have to pay for a more intense (but highly targeted) audit and inspection regime.

However, CPA was mentioned by relatively few respondents in the survey.

2.6 E-government   The Government has set all public services, including local government, the target of achieving 100 per cent electronic service capability by 2005. A willingness to exploit the potential of new technologies will be vital in meeting customer expectations of high quality public services and responding to the needs of local communities. The strategy envisages that all local services will be:

- accessible at times and places most convenient to customers who will have more choice over the way in which they contact and receive public services: through interactive digital TV, through personalised websites, using smartcards, over the telephone, or over the counter

- delivered jointly though outlets hosted by local authorities, government departments or agencies, or through local facilities such as post offices or shops

- delivered seamlessly so that customers only provide the information once

- open and accountable so that information about the objectives, standards and performance of local service providers will be freely and easily available.

Although only nine per cent of public sector managers overall cited "Delivering services online" as a current key challenge (see Appendix 2), responses varied quite sharply by sector. Unsurprisingly respondents working in the Army, Navy or RAF thought themselves far less likely to have to meet this challenge, compared with 17 per cent of those from London/Metropolitan Boroughs, 16 per cent in Executive Agencies and 15 per cent of Civil Service managers. These latter figures suggest either successful implementation of online delivery or, more realistically perhaps, a high level of unpreparedness.

A more general question (see Section 3) asked managers whether they considered "Exploiting the potential of new technologies" was a key skill that those leading public sector organisations should possess.

Less than one in five (18 per cent) identified it as such, and only 23 per cent thought that their own senior management team was successful in this regard, which suggests that around three-quarters of public sector organisations are lagging behind in terms of ICT developments.

These findings tend to reflect those of a more detailed survey – *Better Connected 2003* – an annual nationwide survey of local government web activity carried out by the Society of IT Management.

It found that many local authorities in the UK are unlikely to have fully transactional websites by 2005. Less than half expect to achieve the 2005 target – some 15 per cent are instead concentrating on e-enabling the services likely to deliver the greatest benefits. Few authorities currently have the ability to encrypt data or authenticate citizens to handle sensitive or personal data electronically. Around half are now buying goods and services electronically, although around a third are without an ICT security policy.

2.7 Developing quality frameworks

At the outset of this report we started with a summary of the national agenda set by the government with the four principles of reform, namely:

- Establishing a national framework of standards and accountability

- Devolution to local councils to encourage diversity and creativity

- Building local capacity to offer flexibility at the frontline to exploit opportunities and deliver improved services

- Offering more choice for customers

These principles have some inherent potential conflicts. The imposition of standards and regulatory frameworks works directly against a customer-focused approach to service delivery. There is a contradiction in principles and practice between directives that set standards and targets for our schools and hospitals, for example, and key messages that urge these sectors to develop a more commercial perspective towards the delivery of their services. Accountability and quality should not be confused with control and standardisation, yet this is what appears to have taken place in many services across the UK over the past 10 years.

There will always be a heated debate about the role of government in maintaining standards and accountability across the public sector. But the difficulties experienced in recent years across most sectors still ignore the lessons learned in the private sector through quality initiatives, namely:

- Responsibility for quality should ideally lie closest to those with responsibility for a service, i.e. schemes should be designed and maintained by the professionals themselves

- That the role of government is in meta-evaluation, namely making sure that the systems designed and run by professionals actually work. Government also can play a role in enforcing compliance by strengthening the penalties for low quality delivery

- Performance indicators do not by themselves represent a true measure of quality and may act as distractors from the real pursuit of quality, e.g. all effort is expended in manipulating and reaching the KPI targets, not in improving quality

- The quality criteria and the regulatory framework must be as simple and transparent as possible

- The effort involved in maintaining a quality framework must be significantly less than the improvements and benefits the scheme produces

- There has been much time spent on the development government KPIs, PSAs and league tables, yet often they can fly in the face of established knowledge learned the hard way across the private sector.

In particular, for a real quality revolution to take place across the entire public sector, it is clear is that leaders need the courage to give people the freedom to be creative and to make mistakes. Of course essential services must be maintained at all costs, but a common complaint amongst many interviewees was the fact that the real environment had not changed sufficiently to put them on a par with their private sector counterparts.

If we leave aside the issue of standards discussed above and accept the original principles put forward by government of autonomy, flexibility and customer service, then there are some clear implications of such an approach.

This more commercial, customer-focused approach should be reflected in the attributes and the skills expected among those working in the public sector. We would expect to find a high value placed on business acumen, flexibility, resilience, customer-focus, creativity and innovation.

As we will explore in the next section, it is worrying that this is not the case. The attributes looked for reflect a much more traditional view of management and leadership, albeit with an emphasis on enabling and effective communication of the vision. What is also worrying is that those very skills associated with creativity and innovation were placed very low down on the list.

3   A question of leadership

3.1 Current perceptions of public sector leadership

The survey responses showed that only a third of those working in the public sector rated the leadership qualities of their most senior management teams highly, although a higher number of respondents, (44 per cent), rated their line managers accordingly.

Base: 1890 respondents	Most senior management team %	Own line manager %
Low	32	27
Medium	34	27
High	33	44
Don't know/not stated	1	2

Table 13
Quality of public sector leadership demonstrated at different organisational levels

It is disturbing that two-thirds of managers rate the leadership qualities of their most senior team as of low or medium calibre. Many of the intrinsic qualities sought by those in leadership roles are related to creating a relationship with the follower that is dependent on trust and shared values. This relationship and development of shared understanding is more likely to develop when there is regular communication and interaction.

For many public sector managers however (especially those at more junior levels), contact with those at the most senior levels of the organisation tends to be infrequent, and this may have influenced responses as shown in Table 14.

Base: 1890 respondents	All %	Chief Exec %	Director %	Senior %	Middle %	Junior %
Low	32	6	18	34	33	49
Medium	34	19	35	35	36	30
High	33	71	46	30	32	21
Don't know/not stated	1	5	0	0	0	0

Table 14
Quality of leadership demonstrated by most senior management team – by management level

Half of junior managers working in the public sector do not hold their top team in high regard and only 21 per cent rate the leadership qualities they demonstrate highly. One comment referred to the remote nature of the relationship:

"They talk the talk, but really have no understanding of the change that is required. For once they should try to walk the talk." (NHS Trust)

Ratings improved further up the hierarchy, although Table 14 also showed that even 18 per cent of directors were apparently not impressed by their Boards.

The quality of leadership demonstrated by respondents' own line managers was perceived as higher as shown in Table 15.

Base: 1890 respondents	All %	Chief Exec %	Director %	Senior %	Middle %	Junior %
Low	27	16	22	27	29	33
Medium	27	19	24	27	27	30
High	44	35	51	46	43	37
Don't know/not stated	2	29	2	1	1	0

This difference probably arises from the fact of working in closer proximity or being in more regular contact with individuals at this level of the organisation, compared with the most senior team.

Differences in perceptions of leadership quality also emerged between sectors as seen in Table 16.

Table 16
Quality of leadership
demonstrated at
different organisational
levels – by sector

	Central govt.		Local govt.		Health		Education		Forces	
Rating	Line mgr. %	Most senior mgmt. team %	Line mgr. %	Most senior mgmt. team %	Line mgr. %	Most senior mgmt. team %	Line mgr. %	Most senior mgmt. team %	Line mgr. %	Most senior mgmt. team %
Low	26	33	33	38	27	25	33	40	19	20
Medium	25	35	28	34	28	40	23	30	25	33
High	48	31	37	28	43	34	39	29	57	47

In the local government and education sectors, about 40 per cent of respondents had a low perception of the quality of leadership demonstrated by their most senior management team. This may be because stakeholder involvement and the complexity of structures, particularly funding arrangements, often distort a clear leadership vision. However respondents from the Army, Navy and RAF painted a more positive picture. Their ratings, for both line management and the most senior levels, were consistently higher than their counterparts in other sectors, perhaps reflecting the leadership development activities and interdependent team ethos that is essential in a Forces context.

3.2 Key personal attributes

The attributes sought from today's public sector leaders reflect, as anticipated, the current culture of reform. Running a public service organisation is no longer about managing the status quo – it is about managing modernisation during a time of rising expectations from both government, consumers and employees. Public leaders need to be able to make sense of, and to prioritise the challenges that their organisations face.

Perhaps not surprisingly therefore, clarity of vision was placed firmly at the head of the list shown in Table 17 (cited by 66 per cent of public managers), followed by integrity and sound judgement, which were mentioned by about half of the sample.

Base:1890 respondents	Desired attributes of public sector leaders %	Demonstrated by own most senior mgmt. team %	Demonstrated by own line manager %
Clarity of vision	66	35	28
Integrity	52	34	39
Sound judgement	50	25	33
Commitment to people development	49	36	39
Strategic	46	40	23
Decisiveness	39	29	31
Strong values	26	26	26
Knowledgeable	25	44	41
Creative/innovative	20	14	15
Inspiration	18	8	10
Energy	14	23	27
Passion	9	10	10
Resilience	9	24	21
Humility	6	4	11

Table 17
Key leadership attributes desired/demonstrated at different organisational levels

Yet survey respondents are not seeing these attributes closer to home within their own top teams. They are reporting a gap between expectations and experience in the key public leadership attributes of minus 31 for clarity of vision, minus 18 for integrity and minus 25 for sound judgement. Furthermore the top three qualities that they see demonstrated instead are:

• Knowledgeable

• Strategic

• Commitment to people development

Obviously these are worthwhile attributes at any level – indeed direct line managers are also seen by respondents as knowledgeable and committed to people development. However the greatest potential would seem to lie in improving or developing clarity of vision among senior management teams.

There were also some clear differences by sector as shown below.

Base: 1890 respondents	All %	Central govt. %	Local govt. %	Health %	Education %	Forces %
Knowledgeable	44	46	45	47	38	47
Strategic	40	42	37	45	38	42
Commitment to people development	36	39	32	37	34	42
Clarity of vision	35	37	31	40	32	37
Integrity	34	32	34	33	27	40
Decisiveness	29	30	21	30	22	41
Strong values	26	27	21	27	22	31
Sound judgement	25	23	24	23	22	34
Resilience	24	28	30	27	19	18
Energy	23	26	21	26	21	25
Creative/innovative	14	16	14	13	15	12
Passion	10	10	8	13	10	8
Inspiration	8	9	7	8	8	12
Humility	4	3	4	5	5	5

Table 18
Attributes demonstrated by own most senior management team – by sector

Clarity of vision is a key attribute perceived to be lacking in the top team by respondents working in local government and education, while decisiveness and sound judgement seem to be the hallmark of Forces leadership particularly. Strategic thinking is more likely to be demonstrated by senior managers in the health sector. Managers working in local government were also the least likely to report that they saw commitment to people development being demonstrated.

3.3 Key skills   The survey found that the three top desired public leadership skills were communication, engaging employers with a vision of the organisation, and creating an enabling culture as shown in Table 19. However if we look at the differences between sought qualities and actual experience, the "gap" is again considerable for many of the desired skills. For example the gap between the desire for communication skills and the reality demonstrated among respondents' own top teams, was minus 28, for engaging employees minus 27 and for creating an enabling culture minus 33.

Base: 1890 respondents	Public sector leaders %	Own most senior mgmt. team %	Own line manager %
Communication, including listening, skills	63	35	51
Engaging employees with the vision of the organisation	62	35	31
Creating an enabling culture	60	27	34
Formulating and implementing strategy	48	44	30
Working effectively in partnership with the wider community	48	34	22
Leading change initiatives	43	36	36
Team building	31	21	40
Developing customer service strategy	24	31	22
Developing strong political relationships	23	33	20
Leading the innovation process	20	14	16
Exploiting potential of new technologies	18	23	18
Managing contracts/procurement projects	6	23	16

Table 19
Key skills that public sector leaders should possess

Clearly the pattern of skills that public sector managers look for in their leaders is about creating an inclusive culture, in which leadership is shared throughout the organisation as it discovers new operational structures and new ways of working. This skills pattern is also concerned with selling and promoting change internally, and as such reflects the key desired attribute of clarity of vision.

As one manager said:

66 *Without the trappings of authority, you really have to display clear skills of leadership that people instantly respond to, and too many managers rely on the old props of structure and authority to try and get things done.* 99 (Local government)

53

Many managers also stressed the importance of communication skills:

" *(They) have to be brilliant communicators. They have to show people what is possible, to make them feel a big part of the overall scheme and to help them take charge of their own destiny. Command and control no longer works in this environment.* " (Police)

It may be argued that the degree of fundamental change in attitudes and ways of working has been less than the public sector requires as the findings also reveal a gap between expectation and experience of minus 14 for working effectively with the wider community. This is of concern when the research has suggested a pressing need for public leaders to develop the ability to build and manage effective relationships both with politicians and across a diverse range of organisations.

Similarly it is also concerning to find innovation, either in terms of leading processes or in exploiting new technologies, appearing so low on the list of key skills, along with managing new contracts and procurement projects. The reform agenda will be impeded if leaders and managers fail to respond to the need for new and more flexible ways of working and thinking. Furthermore developing a customer service strategy is also positioned in the bottom half of the list, which is noticeable given the increased emphasis on responsiveness to clients reported elsewhere in the survey.

Case Study

The Defence Leadership Centre

By Air Commodore David Anderson

In April 2000 the Modernising Defence People Group report 'Sustaining the Leading Edge' concluded inter alia that operational leadership skills were excellent, but that leadership beyond the operational area (e.g. business leadership) could be improved. The Report also commented on the need for a more structured approach to leadership development. These broad themes were echoed by the Defence Training Review, published in March 2001, which stated in one of the supporting essays that, "operational leadership skills are amongst the Armed Forces' most valuable assets." Nevertheless, the Report recognised the need to "meet demand for improved leadership skills and respond positively to" the Prime Minister's Modernising Government initiative. In response the establishment of a Defence Leadership Centre (DLC) was agreed by the Secretary of State.

The Centre was officially formed on 1 April 2002, and is now well established at Shrivenham, where it is one of the constituent parts of the Defence Academy of the United Kingdom. The DLC is tasked with improving leadership across Defence, focusing beyond the domain of warfighting and in the strategic environment. In fulfilment of this task, the DLC acts as the Departmental focus – both inward and outward looking – for policy and best practice in leadership, and works with Service and civilian personnel authorities to address any perceived deficiencies in leadership development.

The DLC's 'flagship' activity is the Defence Strategic Leadership Programme (DSLP), which is designed for new 1-Star officers (brigadier and equivalent) and Senior Civil Servants within the Ministry of Defence. The DSLP Foundation Week was successfully piloted in November 2002, with the first full programme due to start in late April 2003. The overall aim of the programme is to enhance leadership at the corporate and strategic level across Defence, and consists of a reflective, behaviourally based Foundation Week followed by a choice of modules to suit individuals' developmental requirements.

The modules range from soft skills, through the challenges of strategic thinking and corporate leadership, to management techniques such as coaching and mentoring and project management. The programme is based on research undertaken by the DLC to establish strategic leadership attributes, via literature searches and a survey of the whole target population, as well as a workshop on the Programme aims.

Continued...

… from previous page

The DLC is also currently examining what support can be provided for more senior officers and officials in preparing for, and taking forward, their roles in the ever more complex leadership environment they face. How best to capitalise on the benefits of e-learning is also under consideration, as is the long-term rationalisation of leadership development training.

Work has also begun on the formulation of an overarching Departmental leadership development strategy that takes into account the needs of the Services and the Civil Service, who already have their own development strategies, as well as the Defence Agencies, many of whom also have their own leadership development schemes. The DLC is also working hard, with different partners, to enhance cross-departmental leadership development, and to 'export' MOD's leadership skills to UK plc in general.

In addition to the provision of developmental education and training, the DLC is currently drafting a leadership handbook, which will be a useful aide memoire and reference on leadership philosophy and practice within the Defence environment. Further research is being commissioned to increase understanding of the requirements of leadership in the strategic environment and within the complex and diverse cultures in which we operate.

The results of the Chartered Management Institute survey 'Leading Change in the Public Sector' will provide a most useful addition to this research and aid our understanding of how current leadership in MOD is viewed.

There is more information about the DLC and its work on the Defence Academy website at www.da.mod.uk/DLC

3.4 Leadership development policies

Most managers feel that the development of effective leadership is critical to the future of their service. Most of those interviewed felt that effective leadership was an important issue that needed to be addressed across their organisation. Even those at the highest level were looking for improved leadership throughout the organisation.

However the survey found that across the whole range of public sector organisations, a clear majority had no **fast track development** systems in place, with the exception of the Armed Forces. They have long placed a high emphasis on identifying potential leaders and nearly 80 per cent of respondents identified a system in existence.

Base:1890 respondents	All %	Central govt. %	Local govt. %	Health %	Education %	Forces %
Yes	32	45	10	20	11	79
No	58	49	78	63	78	17
Don't know	6	4	9	11	5	2
Not applicable	4	2	3	7	6	2

Table 20
Existence of a clearly understood system to identify individuals for fast track development

The education and local government sectors fared worse with only 11 and 10 per cent respectively followed by health at 20 per cent. It is surprising that there is low awareness, despite the existence of well-publicised schemes such as the Management Training Programme in the NHS. It may be that managers distinguish between national schemes and local experience.

As we might expect, there was greater awareness of any fast track development system in younger managers under 35, and there were also differences by number of employees i.e. those workplaces with over 200 staff were more likely to have a fast track system in place.

Table 21 shows that nearly two thirds of managers felt that the **opportunities for development operated at all levels**. Local government was the only area where a minority felt this to be the case. The availability of opportunities was linked to the priority placed on leadership development, but not to whether the service was experiencing major reform.

Base: 1890 respondents	All %	Central govt. %	Local govt. %	Health %	Education %	Forces %
Yes	66	63	48	54	71	73
No	31	31	41	40	29	26
Don't know	3	6	11	6	-	1

Table 21
Whether opportunity for development available at all levels

Only about a third of respondents felt that their organisations placed a high **priority on leadership development** (when compared with other strategic objectives or demands on resources). If this perception is accurate, then it suggests that developing leadership potential in individuals is not embedded consistently enough in public sector culture and behaviour – this may well send conflicting messages to managers.

Indeed the organisational priority placed on leadership development was one of the key discriminators used in further analysis of the results (others included area of public sector respondent works in, management level, age, whether major reform had taken place and number of employees at the workplace).

Table 22 below shows the significant impact that priority and commitment to leadership development has on the morale and satisfaction levels of public sector employees i.e. a net change of plus 23 in organisations which give it a high priority, compared with minus 33 in organisations where it is lower on the agenda.

Employee satisfaction/morale Change in past 3 years	All %	Low priority %	Medium priority %	High priority %
Strongly increased	5	2	4	8
Increased	29	18	28	39
No change	29	27	33	28
Decreased	28	37	27	20
Strongly decreased	9	16	6	4
Net change	-3	-33	-1	+23

Table 22
Relationship between employee satisfaction and priority placed on leadership development

This finding is of greater interest when we bear in mind that 44 per cent of respondents consider that morale among public sector managers is lower than that experienced by their private sector counterparts (see Section 1).

Employee satisfaction/morale Change in past 3 years	All %	Central govt. %	Local govt. %	Health %	Education %	Forces %
Strongly increased	5	4	4	6	4	6
Increased	29	28	27	32	24	35
No change	29	33	30	25	27	27
Decreased	28	28	29	30	29	28
Strongly decreased	9	6	10	6	14	3
Net change	-3	-2	-8	+2	-15	+10

Table 23
Relationship between employee satisfaction and priority placed on leadership development – by sector

Furthermore the two sectors which recorded the greatest decrease in morale and satisfaction over the past three years i.e. education and local government as shown in Table 23, are also the two sectors to record the lowest priority on leadership development. This is distinct from the Armed Forces where only 9 per cent of respondents felt that leadership development was given a low priority (see Table 24) and which reported the greatest positive change in satisfaction and morale over the past three years.

Base:1890 respondents	All %	Central govt. %	Local govt. %	Health %	Education %	Forces %
Low	36	34	45	37	48	9
Medium	30	34	36	35	25	16
High	34	32	20	29	26	75

Table 24
Priority organisation places on leadership development – by sector

Roughly one half of organisations had an explicit budget for leadership development, with local government (38 per cent) and health (40 per cent) faring worst in the league tables. The existence of a budget was linked to the impact of major reform and to the priority placed on leadership development. High priority on leadership was three times more likely to result in a specific budget, and this was also more likely with larger organisations.

Base:1890 respondents	All %	Central govt. %	Local govt. %	Health %	Education %	Forces %
Yes	49	49	38	40	49	68
No	34	32	44	39	36	18
Don't know	14	18	15	17	12	9

Table 25
Whether organisation has an explicit budget for leadership development – by sector

Many respondents across all sectors felt that the resources allocated to leadership development were inadequate.

Base:1890 respondents	All %	Central govt. %	Local govt. %	Health %	Education %	Forces %
Yes	25	28	18	13	26	46
No	50	44	56	62	51	34
Don't know	17	21	18	15	18	12

Table 26
Whether budget for leadership development is adequate – by sector

Only 25 per cent of managers felt the budget was sufficient, and in health and local government this fell to 13 per cent and 18 per cent respectively. In both sectors, a clear majority of managers felt the budget was inadequate. Respondents from the Armed Forces stood out again from the rest of their contemporaries with just under half feeling that the budget was adequate.

Performance appraisal is now a mainstream process in 80 per cent of organisations, but needs to be linked more obviously to leadership development.

Base:1890 respondents	All %	Central govt. %	Local govt. %	Health %	Education %	Forces %
Yes	80	93	72	68	76	97
No	17	6	25	28	19	2
Don't know	2	1	2	1	4	0
Not applicable	1	0	1	2	1	0

Table 27
Whether have regular performance appraisal (at least annually) – by sector

Local government and health were the sectors with the lowest uptake, although two-thirds of all managers did still have an annual appraisal. Central government and the Armed Forces had almost total coverage in their application of an appraisal system.

Despite the fact that best practice in appraisals should be linked to the existence of **personal development plans**, a lower proportion of managers had personal plans in place than had appraisals. Perhaps surprisingly, education fared worst with a little more than half of managers reporting a PDP.

Base:1890 respondents	All %	Chief Executive %	Director %	Senior %	Middle %	Junior %
Yes	65	49	63	64	68	66
No	30	42	31	32	27	28
Not applicable	2	5	3	2	2	1

Table 28
Whether have personal development plan – by management level

There were also clear differences by management level, with only half of Chief Executives and two-thirds of Directors reporting that they had their own development plan in place.

National College for School Leadership (NCSL)

By Professor Geoff Southworth, Director of Research

Launched in November 2000, the College provides professional development and support to English school leaders at all levels and stages of their career. With around 25,000 schools nationally, this represents an estimated client base of around 250,000 people.

The College is predicated on the belief that all children have the potential to become successful learners and that schools play a fundamental role in creating and sustaining the confidence and energy children need to be prepared for the future. Our role in helping to realise this vision is to inspire, challenge and support leaders to be the best they can be to develop leaders who have the vision, skills, passion and energy to transform our schools and to change lives.

Working in partnership with school leaders and the wider education community, the College aims to:

- provide a single national focus for school leadership development, research and innovation

- be a driving force for world-class leadership in our schools and the wider community

- provide support to and be a major resource for school leaders

- stimulate national and international debate on leadership issues

To achieve this, we work in four key areas.

The College is the main driver of research into school leadership in the country, responsible for the commissioning and completion of a wide range of leadership related projects. We are also actively involved in identifying and sharing understanding and knowledge through a range of networks, nationally and internationally.

Through our online work, NCSL provides a range of e-learning opportunities to school leaders. Central to these is the facilitation of online communities – confidential, closed communities where leaders can learn from and with other professionals with similar interests.

We run a range of programmes that support and develop leaders in each of five stages of school leadership (these stages range from emergent leaders at the beginning of their management and leadership responsibilities, through to highly experienced consultant leaders).

Continued…

... from previous page

Many of our programmes recognise the distinctive characteristics of schools, as well as the specific needs of the individual leader.

Furthermore our Networked Learning Communities are designed to capitalise upon and celebrate the diversity that exists within the education system. By working in interdependent and mutually supportive ways, groups of schools have formed learning networks and are using the diversity present within and across institutions as a positive force for knowledge-sharing and innovation.

The NCSL's Learning and Conference Centre in Nottingham provides a state of the art learning resource. However we also work through a network of affiliated centres to provide localised support for leaders.

There is much in this report that resonates strongly with the views of the College.

The need for a framework for ongoing professional development for leaders is highlighted in the report and is central to the fundamental purpose of the College. As noted above, the identification of five distinct stages of school leadership provides a model for considering the specific demands leaders face at each point in their careers, and a pathway for the provision of ongoing support. The establishment of the College sends a critical message to the school leaders profession – they are valued. Professional development is viewed not as a luxury for our school leaders but rather as a right.

The demands placed on leaders are enormous. The report notes evidence of initiative fatigue and target overload among leaders in all areas of the public sector and the associated worries over work-life imbalance that these bring. Arguably these issues are of particular concern for leaders in schools, where the introduction of new programmes, approaches to funding and targets has been most marked. As the College continues to work towards the establishment of a coherent programme of support that addresses the challenges faced at each phase of a school leader's career, the introduction of the Bursar Development Programme for school managers and bespoke seminars focused on individual aspects of work-life balance, are evidence of efforts that have been made to help address these concerns.

The principle that real value comes from a greater distribution of leadership than has traditionally been seen in organisations is a central message of the report and a core tenant of the College's ethos. Distributed leadership is not something that is "done" by a leader or manager, but is rather the creation of an environment where a wider group of individuals is engaged in concerted action that constitutes more than the sum of its parts. In schools, as indeed in all organisations, leaders are most effective when working through others – when they rely not just on the power of one but are

Continued...

able to draw on the power of everyone. All of the National Programmes for leadership development place attention on the importance of encouraging the distribution of leadership within our schools, including amongst students themselves, and are based upon the fundamental belief that it is right to develop and empower leaders outside of the traditional core leadership team.

The call in the report for more flexible and creative approaches to leadership is echoed by the College. NCSL is involved in several initiatives which seek to encourage leaders to reflect on the role they play in facilitating creativity in schools and help them to address the challenges and opportunities that education faces in the future.

Finally, while NCSL is of course a sector specific initiative, we are actively working to learn as much as we can from outside of education and outside of the UK itself. We have established formal mechanisms for linking into business school thinking and our Governing Council is made up of members of the business and school sectors, as well as individuals from the wider policy forum.

Further information on the work of the NCSL can be found on our website at www.ncsl.org.uk

3.5 Methods for developing public sector leaders

As shown in the table, the methods used to develop leaders are diverse and the extent of training experienced is relatively high.

Base: 1890 respondents	Effective for public sector %	Organisation uses %	Personally experienced %
Structured training programmes	56	60	50
Short courses	54	84	76
Mentoring	52	50	35
Project management	49	52	40
Secondment to another organisation	48	38	12
Other postgraduate qualifications	41	45	37
Coaching	40	32	26
360 degree feedback	38	28	27
Action learning teams	37	28	26
Cross functional working	37	32	28
Staff college / internal residential	37	43	37
MBA	35	30	18
Job shadowing	32	28	13
Voluntary/community projects	23	21	12

Table 29
Leadership development methods used in public sector

Overall, 55 per cent of managers have confidence that their training has equipped them for their current role, compared to 16 per cent who were not. There were no significant variances across sectors, although junior managers felt slightly less prepared (21 per cent against 16 per cent overall).

Base:1890 respondents	All %	Chief Executive %	Director %	Senior %	Middle %	Junior %
Very confident	21	33	20	21	23	18
Confident	34	27	37	31	36	33
Neutral	28	23	32	30	25	26
Not very confident	10	6	5	12	9	13
Not at all confident	6	6	4	5	6	8

Table 30
Whether confident that training provided has equipped for current role – by management level

The table below shows variations by management level in terms of training and development personally experienced.

Base:1890 respondents	All %	Chief Executive %	Director %	Senior %	Middle %	Junior %
Short courses	76	80	75	79	75	73
Structured training programmes	50	57	51	49	52	47
Project management	40	47	54	47	35	18
Staff college/internal residential course	37	46	41	40	34	30
Mentoring	35	47	39	36	33	29
Cross-functional working	28	35	43	31	24	14
360 feedback	27	37	39	31	21	18
Action learning teams	26	35	30	29	22	16
Coaching	26	37	29	26	25	22
MBA	18	18	26	23	13	7
Job shadowing	13	19	7	11	14	18
External secondment	12	18	20	12	11	4
Voluntary/community projects	12	24	11	12	12	9

Table 31
Training and development personally experienced – by management level

Seniority has an effect on access to leadership development opportunities. Less formal methods of development such as mentoring and coaching are far more prevalent at the higher levels of the organisation. Junior managers are also apparently missing the opportunity of learning through project management and cross-functional working.

Although a wide range of techniques is used as shown in Table 29, over half of respondents chose formal classroom-based methods as the most effective means of developing leaders in the public sector. Such programmes deliver the basic input of knowledge and best practice thinking that managers need. This is slightly at odds however with the views expressed by interviewees who clearly identified more subtle means of identifying and developing the emerging public sector skills set defined earlier in this section. It is also at odds with private sector organisations. Many have been forced to alter their leadership model radically and are now applying some very sophisticated methods for developing their teams, often at an informal level. This is one of the reasons for the growth in executive coaching, action learning initiatives and e-learning support for leadership development.

Our survey shows that the five methods perceived as most effective for developing public leaders were:

- structured training programmes
- short courses
- mentoring
- project management
- secondment to another organisation.

The five least effective techniques were:

- cross-functional working
- staff college
- MBAs
- job shadowing
- voluntary or community projects.

Structured development programmes often use key projects to drive through the training objectives. Given the extensive change that is taking place in the public sector, it is hardly surprising that these programmes are cited as effective by over half of managers. In contrast 76 per cent of public sector managers had experienced short courses, although only 54 per cent identified this method as an effective way of developing public sector leaders. Perhaps their role in offering basic inputs of knowledge and best practice is seen as valuable, while not being perceived as effective in developing the more sophisticated communication skills required of today's public leaders?

Furthermore a number of methods had a "positive image" bias in that they were perceived as effective by a higher proportion of managers than had actually experienced them – they include secondment to another organisation, job shadowing and mentoring.

For example only 12 per cent of managers have actually experienced an external secondment despite 48 per cent identifying this as an effective leadership development method. Over half of respondents cited mentoring as effective, while around one in three have actually experienced it. Mentoring has increased in popularity as a leadership development tool, as in the private sector. There are some important factors in the uptake of mentoring. In some sectors, its increased use is partly due to the role of mentors in vocational qualification (VQ) development programmes, in others it may arise from a national scheme (e.g. the NHS) to support individual development.

Mentoring schemes are generally informal, and in some cases no more than supplying a list of names to an individual. The factors for success in the development of mentor schemes seem to be similar to the patterns found in other schemes; namely, that effective schemes require the right enabling and co-operative culture to be built up, that mentoring schemes take time and energy to work well, that mentors and mentees both have to want the scheme to work and to invest the energy required, and that mentors require a sophisticated set of skills to work effectively. All interviewees confirmed the powerful influence an effective mentoring scheme can have on organisations.

Coaching, while lower on the list, is nevertheless increasing in significance. It is commonly seen in the same light as mentoring, although coaching for performance as is found in some top companies is a very different animal. In fact, the references to coaching mentioned by interviewees nowhere approached the levels of sophistication found in top companies when developing senior managers. One reason for this may be the high cost commanded by executive coaches. Nevertheless in a number of interviewees, we found a positive interest in the potential offered by this technique and a recognised need to develop coaching skills to improve team performance.

The challenge for many public organisations is to move away from a reliance on traditional and formalised methods of development, and to move towards those methods which are valued as more effective. Their focus is on the impact of individual behaviours and on building time for reflection and feedback.

Personal Perspective

Recruitment for change in the public sector

By Dr Elizabeth Haywood, KMC Consultants

The Research Councils provide a number of interesting examples of change, in that the process is evolutionary with new targets emerging as the more urgent ones are achieved. A personal view on some of these and the different leadership styles that have been employed to achieve change follows.

Background

Each year the Research Councils route about £2 billion of public funding into universities and academic research establishments. They are independent bodies, each with their own Royal Charter, but depend upon Government for funding. The present structure was established following the 1993 White Paper "Realising our Potential" and in response to a perception that the previous arrangements had become ossified and insufficiently responsive to national needs.

Each research council has a Chief Executive reporting to a council and a wide measure of statutory independence. However, the government oversight is via the Director General of Research Councils (DGRC), located in the Office of Science and Technology and reporting to the Permanent Secretary of the Department of Trade and Industry. This DGRC was a new appointment in 1993 with the object of ensuring that the national (as opposed to a more specifically sectoral) interest was addressed.

The first round of changes

Given the statutory independence of the RCs, it was not clear how this remit could be delivered. The first DGRC, Sir John Cadogan, provided strong leadership and did not allow his voice to be disregarded. He made it clear that he was prepared to use his powers, including acting as an intermediary with HM Treasury on funding matters, to ensure attention to the broader agenda. Typically, one RC Chair of Council said to the Chief Executive "regard me as your boss and the DGRC as your customer".

Sir John was a very distinguished academic scientist who had gone on to run the research activities of BP. His leadership led to a change of behaviour that was responsive but not yet integrative. He was also accused by some of being authoritarian – but perhaps he had no choice?

The second round

Cadogan's successor as DGRC was John Taylor who had headed much of the R&D in Hewlett Packard. He inherited a situation in which the RCs listened to the DGRC and took note, but were still jealous of their own territory. As it happened, some of

Continued...

the most interesting developments in science are happening at the interface of the traditional disciplines, and hence of the RCs. Traditionally, these tended to be neglected or the subject of turf war. John Taylor increased the emphasis upon interdisciplinary research and the development of collaborative programmes.

He did this through bringing the CEs of the RCs together to a greater degree than previously, and by encouraging them to think about needs and opportunities in science at a national level, rather than at a disciplinary one. Two management traits have been apparent. Firstly, he encourages and rewards collaborative behaviour – team working. Secondly, he refused to provide the answers to all of the questions, forcing the CEs to come up with their own.

The last manifestation of this process has been the establishment of Research Councils UK (RCUK) as a vehicle to promote collaboration.

The next steps

However the agenda of RCUK could be more radical than the encouragement of collaboration.

There are seven RCs with seven administration systems, seven computer systems, seven public relations machines and so forth. Not only is this costly but the standards of the back up support varies enormously. A second consequence of this distinction is that academics who work across disciplines and need to apply to more than one RC for funding can find themselves having to get used to different rules, different criteria and different paperwork.

The RCs are legally independent and jealous of their role in developing criteria and processes for research funding that are fine tuned to their own research communities. However, under the umbrella of RCUK, the issues of identifying where and how increased use of common services and standards can benefit the system as a whole are now being tackled.

The mere fact that a subject that used to be so sensitive is now firmly on the agenda is a consequence of leadership that has built trust and confidence.

Appendices

Appendix 1

Making a difference in your organisation

How can you start addressing the issues raised by the findings?

Your organisation may have leadership development in place, but does it focus on what really motivates you and affect how you behave?

Good leaders offer their followers a richer experience that stimulates leadership across the board. Based on the research findings, here are some attitudes and behaviours that were reported by managers who **had** experienced effective leadership within teams and across their organisation as a whole.

Why not take some time to reflect on your own leadership style, the leadership you see demonstrated in your organisation and your experiences of leadership development?

For each of the 15 statements following, consider to what extent these behaviours apply to you and your organisation.

1 RATING YOURSELF AS A LEADER

- I view my team as a powerhouse of new ideas and creativity

- I actively manage the political dimension when developing strategic partnerships

- I demonstrate that I am continually learning from those around me

- I can move others towards desired goals despite opposition

- I can recall, within the last week, giving positive feedback to a colleague or team member

2 RATING LEADERSHIP IN YOUR ORGANISATION

- Colleagues are willing to support activities outside of their agreed responsibilities

- I can recall a recent occasion when team members celebrated success and had fun together

- If mistakes are made, we learn from the experience rather than blame others

- There is a challenging environment that supports experimentation and risk-taking

- Our team shares a clear vision of our organisation's future and we trust the top team to get us there

3 RATING LEADERSHIP DEVELOPMENT

- High potential employees are attracted to work for my organisation

- Colleagues are confident that their development equips them for specific leadership roles

- Team members recognise the value of new projects and the learning benefits that result

- Any colleague would be able to discuss how their development plan improves their performance

- I can recall when my views, as a "follower", were actively sought in assessing leadership performance

Appendix 2

Profile of respondents

Base: 1,890

The typical public sector manager is a senior manager, male, aged 45-54 and lives in the south of the country. The majority of managers surveyed have fewer than 200 employees working at their place of work. Fifty-five per cent have been with their current employer for over 10 years, although 55 per cent have also worked in the private sector before. A more detailed profile of respondents is illustrated below.

Age	%
Under 25	2
25-34	11
35-44	27
45-54	41
55-64	18

Gender	%
Male	74
Female	26

Region	%
South East	19
South West	14
London	12
North West	10
Yorkshire/Humberside	8
West Midlands	7
East Anglia	6
East Midlands	6
Scotland	5
North East	4
Wales	4
Northern Ireland	3
Channel Islands	1

Number of employees	At workplace %	Whole organisation %
0-199	53	9
200-499	19	10
500-999	11	11
1,000-4,999	14	19
5,000-9,999	2	11
Over 10,000	0	38

Management level	%
Chief Executive	4
Director	11
Senior manager	39
Middle manager	35
Junior manager	11

Appendix 3

List of interviewees

The Chartered Management Institute conducted 32 telephone interviews with individual members currently working in a wide variety of public service organisations. The authors would like to give special thanks to all those managers who took part in the interviews.

Jim Barrett
Gordon Brakewell
Graham Brown
Jill Bungay
Barry Coker
D M Dalzell
Flight-Lieutenant R Davidson
Peter Dowse
Mark Flynn
Dr Michael Garnett
Hugh Grant
Gavin Greenfield
Lynne Hall
Jenny Heath
R Huskinson
Lynne Lockyer
Paul Marriott
Bethan Norfor
Gail Norris
Tom Norwood
G A Paterson
Ian Piper
Robert Pritchard
Philip Revill
Paul Robbins
Helen Singleton
Trevor Smale
Hilary Stratford
Inspector David Wales
Paul Walker
Peter Allen-Williams
Professor Les Worrall

Appendix 4

Annotated questionnaire

November 2002
Base: 1890

**LEADING CHANGE IN THE
PUBLIC SECTOR** *(All figures in %)*

1   **Which of the following best describes the part of the public
    sector that you work in?**

Central government

Civil service (including devolved administrations)	9
Executive Agency	4
Non-departmental public body	4

Local government

District Council	7
County Council	5
Unitary Authority	6
London/Metropolitan Borough	5

Public sector services

Health	
– NHS Trust	10
– Health authority	1
– Practice management	1
– Other NHS	1
Education	
– Schools	2
– Further education	6
– Higher education	7
– Other *(please specify)*	1
Social services	4
Police	0
Fire	2
Prisons	3
Army	10
Navy	2
RAF	5
Other *(please specify)*	1

A CURRENT CHALLENGES IN THE PUBLIC SECTOR

2 How far has your organisation's culture and values changed over the past THREE years in its emphasis on...?

	Strongly increased	Increased	No change	Decreased	Strongly decreased
Working for public good	13	44	36	4	0
Focus on delivery targets	42	46	10	1	0
Accountability	25	49	21	2	0
Ethics/integrity	12	34	45	6	1
Responsiveness to clients	18	51	25	4	1
Employee satisfaction and motivation	5	29	29	28	9
Improved client satisfaction	11	45	36	6	0
Forming relationships with strategic partners	26	52	19	1	0
Public involvement in service delivery/design	12	42	41	2	1
Influence/involvement of elected authority members	8	25	57	5	1

3 Which are the THREE greatest challenges currently facing you as a public sector manager?

Level of resources/manpower	63
Issues of work-life balance	43
Increase in personal job responsibilities	40
Focus on outcomes rather than inputs	35
Statutory inspection regimes	28
Level of support from above	23
Uncertainty about future career	21
Managing innovation and creativity	18
Personal growth and development	14
Delivering services online	9

4a Has your organisation introduced any major reforms that have directly improved service delivery in the past three years?

Yes   56

No   36

Don't know   8

4b If YES, please describe briefly below.

....

....

....

....

....

B YOUR ROLE AS A MANAGER

5a How far do you think that your own managerial autonomy has increased or decreased over the past THREE years in these areas...?

	Strongly increased	Increased	No change	Decreased	Strongly decreased	Not applicable
Power to resist inappropriate political interference	1	10	49	23	10	7
Input into strategy or policy decisions	8	44	28	15	4	1
Power to influence political decisions	2	16	49	15	7	10
Budgetary autonomy	3	24	44	16	7	5
Power to respond to clients' needs	6	42	35	11	2	2
Setting performance objectives	12	49	27	9	2	1
Power to develop strategic external alliances	11	36	38	7	2	6
Ability to create and develop teams	11	40	36	10	2	1

5b **Please use the space below for any further comments on the issues raised in Question 5a about managerial autonomy.**

....
....
....
....
....

6 **Which, if any, of the following performance improvement initiatives...**

a) Are already in place in your organisation?

b) And which ONE has had the greatest impact?

c) And which ONE has had the least impact?

	(a) Already in place (Tick all applicable)	(b) Greatest impact (Tick ONE only)	(c) Least impact (Tick ONE only)
ISO 9001(quality)	29	5	6
Investors in People	72	11	26
Business Excellence Model (EFQM)	29	5	6
Charter Mark	22	2	5
BS EN 12973 (value mgmt.)	1	0	0
Individual performance-related pay	29	4	9
Group-based performance payments	7	1	2
Statutory inspection regimes	64	29	7
Beacon recognition	14	1	5
Service delivery targets	68	25	5
None of these	3	4	11

7a   **In general, what have been the BENEFITS gained by your organisation from implementing the performance improvement initiative(s)?**

Improved service delivery	50
Enhanced focus on clients needs	57
Increased client satisfaction	26
Greater operational flexibility	19
Increased employee motivation	19
Increased employee productivity	19
More effective communication	36
Increased employee ownership of organisation strategy	23

7b   **In general, what have been the BARRIERS to implementing these performance improvement initiative(s) in your organisation?**

Clash with other initiatives	36
Emphasis on short-term goals	41
Perceived as just another management fad	46
Lack of commitment from the top	25
Lack of training	26
Resistance from employees	30
Too time-consuming and bureaucratic	46
Work pressures	63
Insufficient finance	46
No barriers experienced	2

8   **Please use the space below for any further comments on the issues raised in Question 7 about performance improvement initiatives.**

....
....
....
....
....

C PERSPECTIVES ON LEADERSHIP

9 **Does your organisation have a clearly understood system which identifies individuals with leadership potential for fast track development?**

Yes	32
No	58
Don't know	6
Not applicable	4

10 **If YES, is this opportunity for development available at all levels?**

Yes	66
No	31
Don't know	3
Not applicable	0

11 **How effective is your organisation's approach to encouraging diversity in representation at the most senior levels from...?**

	Good	Average	Poor	Don't know	Not applicable
Women	43	35	13	7	2
Ethnic minorities	32	35	22	6	3
People with disabilities	20	30	28	8	12

12 **What priority does your organisation place on leadership development? i.e. compared with other strategic objectives, or demands on resources**

16	19	30	19	15
Low		Medium		High

13 Is there an explicit budget in your organisation for training and developing its leaders?

Yes   49

No   34

Don't know   14

Not applicable   3

14 Do you think the organisation's budget for training and developing its leaders is adequate?

Yes   25

No   50

Don't know   17

Not applicable   7

15 Do you personally have...?

	Yes	No	Not applicable
A regular performance appraisal e.g. at least annually	80	17	2
A personal development plan	65	30	2
Access to an open internal job market	62	21	13

16 How confident are you that the training and development provided by your organisation has equipped you for your current role?

Very confident   21

Confident   34

Neutral   28

Not very confident   10

Not at all confident   6

17 **Thinking about the sorts of training and development in leadership that are available nowadays, which of the following...**

a) Does your organisation make use of?

b) Have you ever personally experienced?

c) Do you think are effective in developing public sector leaders?

	(a) Organisation uses	(b) Personally experienced	(c) Effective for public sector
Action learning teams*	28	26	37
Cross-functional working	32	28	37
360° feedback	28	27	38
Mentoring	50	35	52
Coaching	32	26	40
Short courses	84	76	54
Structured training programmes	60	50	56
MBA	30	18	35
Other postgraduate qualifications	45	37	41
Staff college/internal residential course	43	37	37
Secondment to another organisation	38	12	48
Voluntary/community projects	21	12	23
Project management	52	40	49
Job shadowing	28	13	32
None of these	2	2	1

*which tackle significant internal projects or problems

18a **How would you rate the quality of the leadership demonstrated by the most senior management team in your organisation?**

15	17	34	23	10
Low		Medium		High

18b   And how would you rate the quality of leadership demonstrated by your own line manager?

13	14	27	28	16
Low		Medium		High

19   Which are the FIVE key personal attributes...

a) That public sector leaders in general should possess?

b) That members of the most senior management team in your organisation demonstrate?

c) That your own line manager demonstrates?

	(a) Public sector leaders in general	(b) Own most senior mgmt. team	(c) Own line manager
Clarity of vision	66	35	28
Commitment to people development	49	36	39
Creative/innovative	20	14	15
Decisiveness	39	29	31
Energy	14	23	27
Humility	6	4	11
Integrity	52	34	39
Inspiration	18	8	10
Knowledgeable	25	44	41
Passion	9	10	10
Resilience	9	24	21
Sound judgement	50	25	33
Strategic	46	40	23
Strong values	26	26	26

20   Which THREE public sector leaders do you most admire?

1 ....

2 ....

3 ....

21 Which are the FIVE key skills...

a) That public sector leaders in general should possess?

b) That members of the most senior management team in your organisation demonstrate?

c) That your own line manager demonstrates?

	(a) Public sector leaders in general	(b) Own most senior mgmt. team	(c) Own line manager
Creating an enabling culture	60	27	34
Communication, incl. listening skills	63	35	51
Developing customer service strategy	24	31	22
Developing strong political relationships	23	33	20
Engaging employees with the vision of the organisation	62	35	31
Exploiting potential of new technologies	18	23	18
Formulating and implementing strategy	48	44	30
Leading change initiatives	43	36	36
Leading the innovation process	20	14	16
Managing contracts/ procurement projects	6	23	16
Team building	31	21	40
Working effectively in partnership with the wider community	48	34	22

CLASSIFICATION

22 How long have you...

a) Worked for your current employer and

b) Been in your current job with your current employer?

	(a) With current employer	(b) In current job
Less than 1 year	6	21
1-3 years	16	40
4-6 years	12	17
7-10 years	10	8
Over 10 years	55	11

23 Have you ever worked in the private sector?

Yes	55	No	44

24 As a public sector manager, how do you think the following compare with your counterparts in the private sector?

	Better	Same	Worse	Don't know
Loyalty to employer	48	31	15	6
Morale	15	35	44	6
Motivation	23	34	36	6
Perceived job security	59	27	9	5

Appendix 5

Bibliography

Audit Commission (2003) *Patterns for Improvement – Learning from comprehensive performance assessment to achieve better public services*

Audit Commission (2002) *Recruitment and Retention – A public service workforce for the twenty-first century*

Audit Commission (2001) *Changing Gear – Best value annual statement 2001*

Audit Commission (2000) *Aiming to Improve: the principles of performance measurement*

CBI Policy Unit (2002) *CBI Recommendations for the 2002 Government Spending Review*

HM Treasury (2003) *Public Services: Meeting the productivity challenge*

HM Treasury (2002) *Cross-cutting Review of the Public Sector Labour Market*

National Expenditure and Income Division, Office for National Statistics (2002) *Measuring Productivity Change in the Public Sector*

Office of National Statistics (2002) *Civil Service Statistics 2001*

Public Administration Select Committee (2002) *The Public Service Ethos: Government's response to the committee's seventh report of session 2001-02*

The Employers' Organisation (EO) in association with Deloitte & Touche (2002) *Productivity, Performance and Improvement*

The Performance and Innovation Unit (2001) *Strengthening Leadership in the Public Sector*

The Prime Minister's Office of Public Services Reform (2002) *Better Government Services – Executive agencies in the 21st century*

The Prime Minister's Office of Public Services Reform (2002) *Reforming our Public Services – Principles into practice*

Attwood, M et al. (2003) *Leading Change – A guide to whole systems working*

Charlesworth, K, The Institute of Management (2000) *A Question of Quality – A survey of performance improvement in the UK*

Crouch, C (2003) *Commercialisation or Citizenship – Education policy and the future of public services*

Donovan, N & Brown, J & Bellulo, L, Performance and Innovation Unit, Cabinet Office (2001) *Satisfaction with Public Services: A Discussion Paper*

Escott, K & Whitfield, D, The Equal Opportunities Commission (2002) *Promoting Gender Equality in the Public Sector*

French, S & Marsden, D, Centre for Economic Performance (1998) *What a Performance – Performance related pay in the public services*

Horne, M & Steadman Jones, D, The Institute of Management (2001) *Leadership: the challenge for all?*

Kelly, G & Stephen, M, Strategy Unit, Cabinet Office (2002) *Creating Public Value - An analytical framework for public services reform*

Mabey, C & Thomson, A, The Institute of Management (2000) *Achieving Management Excellence – A survey of UK management development at the millennium*

Makinson, J, Public Services Productivity Panel (2000) *Incentives for Change: rewarding performance in national government networks*

Talbot, C, The Institute of Management (1994) *Reinventing Public Management – A survey of public sector managers' reactions to change*

Continued...

Journal articles

Allison, M & Hartley, J (2000) *The role of leadership in the Modernisation and Improvement of Public Services*, Public Money and Management, April-June 2000, Vol. 20, No. 2

Alimo-Metcalfe, B, University of Leeds (1998) *Leadership: feedback counts when it is 360 degree*, Leadership of Management Education

Bichard, M (2000) *Creativity, Leadership and Change*, Public Money and Management, April-June, Vol. 20, No. 2

Boland, T & Fowler, A, University of Newcastle (2000) *A Systems Perspective of Performance Management in Public Sector Organisations*, The International Journal of Public Sector Management, Vol. 13, No. 5

Brookfield, D, University of Liverpool (2000) *Management Styles in the Public Sector*, Management Decision, Vol. 38, No. 1

Boyett, I, University of Nottingham (1996) *The Public Sector Entrepreneur – A definition*, The International Journal of Public Sector Management, Vol. 9, No. 2

Broussine, M, University of West England (2000) *The Capacities needed by Local Authority Chief Executives*, The International Journal of Public Sector Management, Vol. 13, Nos. 6 & 7

Denis, J & Langley, A & Pineault, M (2000) *Becoming a Leader in a Complex Organisation*, Journal of Management Studies 37:8, pp. 0022-2380

Huxham, C & Vangen, S, University of Strathclyde (2000) *Leadership in the Shaping and Implementation of Collaboration Agendas: how things happen in a (not quite) joined-up world*, The Academy of Management Journal, Vol. 43 No. 6, pp. 1159-1175

Talbot, C, University of Glamorgan (2001) *UK Public Services and Management (1979-2000) – Evolution or revolution?*, The International Journal of Public Sector Management, Vol. 14, No. 4

Managing High Performance in the Public Sector, IRS Employment Review, No. 690, pp. 5-11 (1999)